**Endorsements for the**

"If you don't know what ra
read "We are All Racists." In this brief but cutting edge
book, Dr. Lewis weaves personal narratives throughout
to tell a clear and concise story of what racism is, what it
looks like, and importantly what can be done about it.
Everyone can take something from this book no matter how
knowledgeable or naive you are on the topic!"

Dr. Faye Belgrave
Professor of Psychology, Virginia
Commonwealth University
Director of the Center for Cultural
Experiences in PreventionCo-Author of African-American
Psychology 3rd Edition (2014)

"This is an outstanding addition to how race is operationalized
and interpreted in America. 'We are All Racists: The Truth
about Cultural Bias' will be among the best sellers. The
personal disclosures offered by Dr. Lewis combined with
both the theoretical and empirical evidence on how race
is operationalized and interpreted in America are truly a
masterpiece of exceptional scholarship. Thus, this book is a
must read for educators, students and laypersons."

Dr. Keith Wilson
Dean, College of Education and
Human Services
Southern Illinois University

"Dr. Allen Lewis has written a brief narrative that both illuminates the nature of racism and cultural bias and offers a series of practical solutions/strategies that can mitigate their personal, cultural, political, and economic costs. His search for analysis and explanation ranges from his personal and familial struggles with race through a succinct review of multiple theories that seek to explain the unexplainable human condition. Lewis concludes that some aspects of the ubiquitous focus on race and culture are partially due to human proclivity to be most comfortable with similarity. He concludes the work with a set of strategies that he terms the "Black Triangle" designed to be an example of how to facilitate healing and forward progress within the African-American community in light of the trauma of racism experienced in this country."

Dr. King Davis
Mike Hogg Professor in Community
Affairs, African and African
Diaspora Studies Department
College of Liberal Arts - University of Texas
at AustinInaugural Director, Institute
for Urban Policy Research & Analysis

"In 1903, as we entered the 20th century, Dr. W.E.B DuBois identified racism as the major issue facing this nation. A century later Dr. Allen Lewis reminds us that the issue is still on the table and that we are all involved. Moving us through the lens of cultural bias and narcissism, he offers a road to healing and empowerment. His book is as readable as it is incisive. It is also a reminder that if we are all a part of the problem, we can also be a part of the solution."

Reverend, Dr. Yvonne V. Delk
Minister and Activist

# WE ARE ALL
# RACISTS

# WE ARE ALL
# RACISTS
## THE TRUTH ABOUT
## CULTURAL BIAS

# Allen Lewis, PhD

YorkshirePublishing
www.yorkshirepublishing.com
*Write Now.*

ISBN: 978-1-949231-50-2
*We are All Racists: The Truth about Cultural Bias*
Copyright © 2014 by Allen Lewis, PhD.

Yorkshire Publishing
3207 South Norwood Avenue
Tulsa, Oklahoma 74135
www.YorkshirePublishing.com
918.394.2665

This book would not have been possible without my immediate family: wife, daughter, and son. They are truly my reason for being. I also owe a debt of gratitude to my biological father (deceased in 1976), my stepfather (who still guides me today), and my mother who has always been everything to me. My mother's recent and sudden death in late 2013 literally stopped me in my tracks. Sadly, I had not spoken to her about this book since I wanted it to be a surprise for her. Now, she has to see it finished from heaven above. Finally, and of utmost importance, I give all praise and honor to my Lord and Savior, Jesus Christ.

# CONTENTS

# PREFACE

This book has been in my subconscious for a while, but the impetus for it now is the racial divide in America on the heels of the acquittal of George Zimmerman in the Trayvon Martin case. The nation's polarized reaction to the verdict makes clear that race is still a defining factor for Americans in the twenty-first century. Americans still view the world through a race lens. This represents a paradox in that we have seen much progress on the one hand. On the other hand, maybe we have not if race is still so important in how we view and interpret the world, and notably we are sixty years after the Brown decision.

Perhaps it is time to face the truth that race and cultural differences may always be the defining prisms through which we all experience our respective realities. Human beings, like other animal species, seem particularly inclined to prefer own kind in terms of cultural characteristics. Now, this is not to say that this natural tendency cannot be overridden, but to do so requires conscious, willful effort. In the absence of such volition, the default is that culturally based preferences and biases, such as race, will prevail.

The good news is that in a pluralistic society like America, we can enjoy both intra- and intercultural experiences. These two realities can coexist, but there must be a better understanding among the masses of the dynamics at play. For without deliberate decision making that only humans can engage in within the animal world, the resulting outcome is that *we are all racists.*

The purpose of this book then is to present the truth about cultural bias in the twenty-first century. That truth is relatively unchanged since the beginning of human existence. However, many are not familiar with this truth, and its relevance now is unprecedented largely due to the expectations of many that we should be beyond such challenges in 2014. It is the dichotomy between expecting that race and other forms of cultural bias are less significant now given our evolution as a society *and* the fact that Americans still seem to have a preoccupation with race that renders this discussion timely.

This is an intentionally brief discussion because I want every American to have the time to be exposed to it amid the hectic pace and competing demands of daily life today. At just over one hundred pages, I think this discussion could be easily read within one or several sittings. The discussion starts with a personal journey that contextualizes, humanizes, and provides some transparency about the origin of my own thoughts about cultural bias, of which racism is only one type. Note: I often use the terms *black* and *white* throughout the text primarily for simplicity and expediency instead of the more politically correct terms of African American and European American.

I hope you enjoy this short read.

Sincerely,
Allen N. Lewis, Jr., PhD

# INTRODUCTION

We are all racists. This is a provocative yet true statement. In this book, I take this position, and what I mean is that racism is an attribute that is universal within the human experience. Therefore, none of us is immune or exempt from it. Cultural bias is a broad concept that often manifests narrowly as racism. It just so happens that racism is the specific type of cultural bias that has plagued the history of the United States since its beginning. The fact that race is a visible form of cultural bias, noticeable at a glance, has served to sustain its relevance for generations. The irony is that much of the scientific evidence has called into question the notion that race is biology, as asserted by anthropologist, Dr. Audrey Smedley, and her son, Brian Smedley, of the Institute of Medicine, in their 2005 article in the journal, American Psychologist, appropriately titled *Race as Biology is Fiction, Racism as a Social Problem is Real: Anthropological and Historical Perspectives on the Social Construction of Race.*

This discussion on race is divided into five chapters beyond this introduction. I start on a personal level, sharing some meaningful experiences early in my own life. These experiences not only illustrate the formation of my own cultural bias, but also show how my developmental progression from childhood to adult life in America shaped the conceptualization of race for me. Next, I discuss pluralism in America and the myriad of relevant cultural dimensions, define culture, provide a working definition of cultural bias, lay out some theoretical origins of bias, talk about the natural human processes that perpetuate bias, and offer some strategies to minimize cultural bias. The subsequent section overviews what the past tells us today, embracing a historical perspective. The next section discusses the healing needed in communities using the black community as an example of broad-based healing that needs to occur. I conclude the discussion by addressing the health imperative in the black community and then look forward to the future by outlining some interesting current societal developments as well as a bit of good news.

# PROFOUND PERSONAL EXPERIENCES

## WASH ME CLEAN!

I clearly remember my mother talking to me as an adult and laughing as she explained how as a young child of about four years old, I went through a "wash me clean" phase. Every time she bathed me, over a period of a few weeks, I would ask her to be sure to wash me clean. My mother thought nothing of it at first since she was a kindergarten teacher and accustomed to preschoolers having a vivid imagination and a propensity for seemingly irrelevant chatter. However, I seemed to be somewhat obsessed with making sure she washed me clean in every bath.

After a while, my mother began to ponder the fact that I had insisted on her washing me clean for several weeks. So one day, after I uttered, "Be sure to wash me clean, Mom," she responded, "But I always wash you clean." I quickly replied, "No, Mom, wash me clean like the kids on *The Sound of Music*" (the movie). This startled my mother at first, but then she immediately knew what was going on.

I loved the movie, *The Sound of Music*, and related to those Von Trapp kids, several of whom were near my age. I wanted so much to be like them, especially their skin color, but at that young age, I had no familiarity with the concept of race. In my four-year-old mind, the difference between the Von Trapp children and me was a matter of cleanliness. It is at that critical point as a young child that the lack of media images that resembled me began to subconsciously negatively influence my self-worth. Some might argue that this was the beginning of internalized oppression or self-hate. In other words, external biases related to race in United States society as manifested in mainstream media were beginning to build a sense of self-deprecation within me on a subconscious level.

## WATCHING THE SUMMER OLYMPICS WITH MY DAD (1972 AND 1976)

My father and I had a close relationship and a tradition of watching sports together on television, especially football, basketball, and the Summer Olympics. This was one of our special father-son bonding activities. I remember my father as one of the smartest, fairest, and down-to-earth men I have ever known. We were especially fond of watching the Summer Olympics. Back then, in the 1970s, Olympic athletes were the best in the world *and* they had amateur status. Our favorite events to watch were the sprints in track and field, basketball, and boxing. We were patriotic and always rooted for the United States athletes, but within this subset, we also always pulled for black athletes to prevail. My father, who by the way was an intellectual, died suddenly of heart failure when I was fifteen.

My father would always explain to me that having racial pride was acceptable to a point. By this, he meant that one should always treat all people fairly despite racial orientation in interpersonal and small group dealings, but it was okay to pull for one's own race in what he called trivial life events like sporting endeavors. My father likened racial pride to patriotism or school pride in that one typically wants own team, school, or country to win even though unfair or mistreatment of rival team members would be intolerable. My father also explained that racial pride is ethnocentricity and that when taken to an extreme (i.e., believing that some groups are inherently or genetically superior or inferior based primarily on biological factors) becomes racism, which he was clear about not being a desirable attribute.

## ELEMENTARY SCHOOL

In elementary school, I had the dual experience of attending two nonintegrated all black schools and one integrated primarily white school. During grades 1 through 4, I attended two public schools that were all black in the late 1960s. In 1971, we relocated to a new city, and I attended an all-white elementary school as a fifth grader. When I arrived at the new school, there was only one other black student already attending, a female fifth grader. I was the first and only male (second black kid) to enroll in the elementary school. In a sense, my fellow black female schoolmate and I were trailblazers for integration at that elementary school. My female compatriot seems to have been blending in well, my assumption since she and I never actually spoke about her experiences. However, for me, things were different.

Acclimating to this new school as the first black male student was a learning experience, though I had no recognition at the time of the magnitude of the lessons I was learning. There appeared to be three types of white male students in terms of their reactions to me. One group of students seemed to be perfectly comfortable with me being in their class. Another group of students appeared to be "on the fence" about me. They were unsure whether to accept me or not. Their acceptance of me swayed with the wind. This group also seemed to be particularly open to influence by one of the other two groups. The final group was a small cadre, and it consisted of two or three boys who were carrying on the tradition of segregation, as they were not about to allow a new black male student to smoothly integrate into their fifth grade class. My teacher appeared to be an open-minded, fair, young white female.

I had several run-ins with the group of boys, who seemingly opposed my being their classmate. For the most part, those instances were annoying nuisance situations that interrupted the flow of the day, but due to my personal resilience and strong self-concept, they did not prohibit the success of my academic experience. Little did I know at the time that I was learning volumes about race, racism, and the integration experience in America. This was also the time in United States history and the South when it was commonplace to see the "little red schoolhouse" stickers that adorned the vehicle bumpers of many white parents who supported neighborhood schools. This strong support for neighborhood schools was a clear disdain for and retrenchment against integration.

So as I continued to go about my business as a fifth grade student, I had occasional disputes with that group of boys that resisted my presence. I recall one particular dispute that was significant. One day, on the playground at recess, we were playing German dodge ball. The ball came my way, but I dodged it cleanly. However, several of my classmates insisted that I was hit and, therefore, out. I stood my ground (sound familiar?). An altercation ensued, and one of my white classmates yelled from across the playground, "You're out, nigger!" He and I had words and ended up in fisticuffs. I did not initiate the brawl, but was sent to the principal's office. I was summarily suspended.

My parents were livid and the next day, they—my mother, the former kindergarten teacher and then accountant, and my father, the college professor—met with the principal and informed him that I was not to initiate trouble, but that if verbal racial insults were targeted to me or if anyone touched me, I was instructed to defend myself. Then, my parents made a preemptive strike and claimed my teacher did not have control of the class if such an incident occurred. At my parents' insistence, I was immediately reinstated in school and do not recall any further overtly racist comments from my classmates for the remainder of the school year. Sure, I am certain the racist innuendos continued, but there were no further outwardly racially motivated altercations for the rest of that year.

## MIDDLE SCHOOL

When I started middle school, I expected more of the same in terms of encountering that faction of students who were opposed to my presence and who were overtly racist. However, in my middle school, I, as a black student, was not nearly as much of a rarity. I was still the only black kid in my sixth grade class, but there were other black students sprinkled lightly throughout other classes and the other two grade levels, seventh and eighth grades. There was even a black teacher, a physical education teacher/coach. Little did I know that I was about to experience my first dose of racism from a teacher, and it was covert racism.

My sixth grade history and English teacher was a Bostonian, and being a Northerner, an unlikely perpetrator of racism, so we thought at the time. She hailed from Harvard University and was so fond of this lineage that she informed every student and parent she met of this fact. The precursor of racism began to rear its ugly head when this teacher established groups of students within the class based on ability. These groups were based on her independent judgment about each student's academic ability. There were three groups: A, B, and C. The A group was for students with superior academic ability, the B group for above average students in terms of academic ability, and the C group was for students with mediocre academic ability. I was initially assigned to the C group to which my parents immediately waged an objection. I was then moved to the B group. To this point in my educational career, I had always been an A–B student. After being moved to the B group at my parent's insistence, my performance in this teacher's eyes was consistently assessed at the C-level. My parents battled her tooth and nail the entire year, questioning her every evaluation of me and my work. My parents were true advocates for me.

I recall one situation as if it happened yesterday. We were assigned a term paper on Mesopotamia, I believe. My father informed me that we were going to conduct an experiment. He said that I would not be doing the paper, but that he would. My dad, the college professor, completed the term paper and I submitted it as my own. The grade I received was the usual C. My parents requested yet another meeting with my teacher. In the meeting, my father questioned the grade and then informed my teacher that she was grading based on preconceived notions of my ability rather than merit. He then revealed that he had in fact completed the paper. She was initially stunned, but then questioned my father's competence, implying that his skills were on a sixth grade C-level. He proceeded to not only call her a racist, but to also let her know that he was a college professor who routinely taught individuals on her level as a bachelor's degree trained teacher.

My father and mother next scheduled a meeting with the school principal to reveal the results of their experiment. Needless to say, this teacher was placed under close scrutiny for the remainder of the year. My grade in this class did improve to the B-level for the rest of the year. The remainder of my time in middle school was much less remarkable, probably because the word had spread about my parents.

## HIGH SCHOOL

When I started high school in the mid-1970s, integration had progressed considerably. Blacks were probably 5–10 percent of my class, and this matched the proportion in the general population of the county at the time. Black teachers were still pretty nonexistent in majority white schools. For example, I do not recall there being one black teacher in my high school.

I was a successful high school student. I did well academically, played a sport, and was a popular kid. Academically, I enrolled in the college preparatory curriculum that included almost all honors and advanced courses. I ran indoor and outdoor track and was a dedicated weightlifter. Years of weightlifting in middle and early high school contributed to me having a heavily muscled physique by my sophomore year in high school.

My popularity manifested mostly among my female peers who were enamored by my physique and whom were mostly white. I sang in an all-white choral ensemble as well. I had many white male friends based on my membership in the Key Club and, of course, many black male and some black female friends. In my junior year, I was selected as one of two male sweethearts for an all-white female club, Triangle II. The other male sweetheart was white.

I do not recall any overt brushes with racism. This could have been because most of my male peers feared me as the most muscular and strongest kid in the school. My nickname was the "Incredible Hulk." I also do not remember any overt or covert racism perpetrated by my teachers. This is probably a good thing since my father had died suddenly the summer after my ninth grade year. My mother was still a formidable advocate for me, but did not possess the ferocity of my father. Though I did not have any glaring evidence of racism perpetrated by my teachers, I did have some suspicions that several of my teachers did not like me because of the color of my skin.

I was always a respectful, mannerly, and smart kid. However, there were several teachers in advanced math and English courses in particular that I felt a cool reception from. I could not put my finger on it and claim definitively that it was racism, but it felt to me that these few teachers felt I did not belong in those advanced classes. The fact of the matter is that I was almost always the lone black student in those accelerated courses. This fact alone may have been evidence of some racism in advisement and course selection in that black students were typically not encouraged to take rigorous and advanced courses. Oftentimes, in those advanced classes where I perceived a cool reception from the teachers, my grades were average. By this time in my development, I was pretty astute at picking up on subtleties like covert racism. At best, I lacked a warm rapport with those few teachers, and at worst, they were racists. I was not able to definitively discern one way or another, but I had my suspicions.

## UNDERGRADUATE EXPERIENCE AT THE UNIVERSITY OF VIRGINIA

I attended the University of Virginia (UVA) from 1979 to 1983. Outside of the immense learning I experienced in the classroom, I gained immeasurable knowledge about cultural matters outside of the classroom. I also learned more about the black experience, the white experience, the experiences of other world cultures from the many international students, and about cross-cultural perspectives, i.e., what happens when diverse viewpoints interface in the same context. I had many varied exposures that were illuminating.

During my first year at UVA, I became friends in the dormitory with black, Latino (Cuban), Asian (Chinese), and white classmates. My closest set of friends initially included a white Cuban American, a Chinese American, an Italian American, a Jewish American, an Irish American, and an African American. We started a singing group called the Rootations (nine guys). This name was significant because it derived from the word *root*. The term *root* was our euphemism for the word *penis*, which we had a healthy (some thought unhealthy) obsession with as eighteen-year-old young men.

The Rootations performed around campus singing in a 1950s and early 1960s genre reminiscent of the group Sha Na Na, performing tunes such as "Barbara Ann," "Teenager in Love," and "Chain Gang." We wore white t-shirts and jeans, had slicked back hair, and had a multiethnic look, choreographed steps, along with respectable voices. We were good enough to win the university-wide student talent show in 1980, which was no small feat at a school the size of UVA and given its diverse and deep talent pool among the student body. The Rootations recorded a call song for the UVA student-run radio station to the tune of the Fifth Avenue candy bar jingle. We had quite a following of first year females. In fact, we formed an all-female contingent of groupies called the Rootettes. This was also a multiethnic, primarily white, cadre of first-year females that adored us and dated us off and on.

Not only were the Rootations best friends and performers, but we were also habitual pranksters and made a mockery of many things around campus. I remember once we decided to mock the black Greek pledge lines. So one evening, we dressed up as a fictitious fraternity that we called Root Phi Root and sauntered around campus for several hours in a pledge line formation chanting, "Root. Root. Root Phi Root. Our boots are heavy, our shirts are tight, our roots are swinging from left to right. Root. Root. Root Phi Root" (repeat).

In my second year at UVA, a subgroup of four of the Rootations lived off campus in a house. We were always a curious and unique bunch of guys from the vantage point of those who knew us from afar. I was arguably the most curious and misunderstood. I dated black and white females. I lived in a house that resembled a miniature United Nations in terms of ethnic diversity. I was a member of the Rootations singing group and a member of the UVA Weightlifting Club. I had a double major in Rhetoric and Communication Studies and African-American and African Studies.

It was not until my third year at UVA that I became a true enigma from the perspectives of both the black and white student communities. In that year, I became very conscious of my black identity. I joined and became an active member of the Black Student Alliance (BSA), a student government and advocacy organization, and adopted a new set of black friends from that organization. At the same time, I maintained my Rootation friends. My nonblack friends were initially puzzled because they knew me as a guy who was fair to everyone and who functioned as if race did not matter. They reasoned that I must have been becoming a black militant by joining the BSA, an organization that at the time was widely misunderstood and viewed as antiwhite. (By the way, the BSA was never antiwhite, just pro equality for blacks. There were, in fact, white members of the BSA.) Admittedly, the BSA had a legacy of staging rallies, protests, and sit-ins and taking hard-line symbolic positions on matters that were often perceived as militant and non-compromising. Additionally, my black friends and BSA affiliates viewed me as not black enough because my closest friends and the people I lived with (i.e., the Rootations) were mostly white. Moreover, I had the audacity to not exclusively date black females. I may not have been black enough in the eyes of black students, but I was about to become blacker.

As I stated previously, the BSA had a reputation for assuming symbolic and non-compromising positions on issues and frequently using nontraditional means such as sit-ins. In this my third year at UVA, I became one of the infamous

"UVA 7." The UVA 7 was a group of seven BSA members who orchestrated a sit-in at a UVA Board of Visitors' meeting, essentially occupying the meeting space and refusing to leave until the board took action to respond to our demands. The Board of Visitors' meeting had to be dismissed before it started because we (the UVA 7) refused to leave. Luckily, we were not arrested, but each one of us was brought up on judiciary charges and faced sanctions up to expulsion from school.

Here are the two demands that the UVA 7 wanted the Board of Visitors to address: (1) improved recruitment and retention of black students and faculty. To obtain enhanced retention of black faculty, we wanted an overhaul of the faculty promotion and tenure process that, at the time, disadvantaged black faculty, we reasoned based on the disproportionately negative outcomes for black faculty who had gone through the process. (2) We wanted to have an active voice in the selection of the new dean of African-American Affairs and not have someone selected in the position without BSA input who would be a figurehead and essentially a yes person to the then almost all-white UVA administration.

Before staging the sit-in, the BSA had voiced and attempted to address these demands directly with the vice president for Student Affairs and the university president, but had been effectively ignored. Given this, we reasoned that the Board of Visitors would afford us a forum to address our concerns. However, the board would not put us on the agenda. Therefore, we staged the sit-in to force the board to address our concerns.

The outcome was that we did not have our demands addressed, and the seven of us student activists who were members of the UVA 7 were almost expelled from school. Proceedings to expel us were thwarted largely due to the groundswell of support from the NAACP, the American Civil Liberties Union (we had heard, but this was not verified), and many other supporters outside of the UVA community, including our parents who initiated a national letter-writing campaign to keep us in school. UVA received some negative publicity in this ordeal for not addressing our concerns and ultimately decided to drop the judiciary charges as a compromise. By the way, our two demands never received adequate attention. This was a major lesson for me about effective system change strategies.

By my fourth year as a UVA student, the mystery about me (i.e., where my allegiances lied) had reached a new high. I had been elected vice president of the UVA Weightlifting Club, an all-white (except me) organization of meat-headed wannabe jocks. I had also been elected president of the BSA. Some actually called the BSA "the Built Student Alliance" after I took over as president because of my well-developed physique. My black friends and BSA affiliates did not understand me having primarily white friends. My white friends did not understand me leading an organization like the BSA. I had also been a member of the notorious UVA 7, further fueling the speculation about what made me tick.

As my presidency of the BSA commenced in my fourth year as a UVA student, I was clear on my agenda. First, I vowed that the BSA would operate under a new philosophy of pragmatism. No longer would we engage in symbolic actions that were long on principle and effort and short on "net gain" improvement. I reasoned that the BSA needed to engage in strategic, net gain activities that truly advanced our mission and did not merely result in taking a stand. I also endeavored to build a broader base of support for the BSA among all UVA students by explaining in clear terms our mission and inviting all students to become involved with the BSA. I strategically surrounded myself with black and white friends to demonstrate that the leader of the BSA was not antiwhite or racist, but merely a fellow UVA student leading an organization that embraced a noble and laudable cause of promoting cultural pluralism, i.e., a level playing field, acceptance, and equality for all students, irrespective of race or ethnicity.

I deployed several more strategies to cast the BSA as an improved, more evolved, and inclusive organization. First, I tracked my sitting patterns whenever I consumed a meal at one of the student dining halls. Because students when dining primarily sat in homogeneous groupings with respect to race, I made a conscious attempt to alternate my seating with black and white student groupings. For example, if I sat with black students for breakfast, I would be sure to sit with white students at lunch, then black students again at dinner, and so on. This allowed me to treat both groups equally since I was a valuable member of both and had valued friendships in both groups.

The second strategy I utilized was to establish a "Bicultural Awareness" month. My original thinking around such an event was to facilitate reciprocal cultural awareness within both the black and white student communities to foster greater mutual understanding between these two groups. We held a series of programs and events throughout the month designed to acquaint students with both cultural viewpoints. We also had a series of panel discussions aimed at bridging differences and promoting cultural respect and humility. Some students thought I had been too narrow in my conceptualization of bicultural in targeting it to a black-white dynamic and broadened bicultural to mean expose your own culture to someone of a different culture and then learn about that person's culture. This worked well for those who made this more individualized comparison, though we did not have formal events so targeted.

The remainder of my tenure as BSA president was positive and uneventful in terms of adversity. The hardcore BSA members who relished the old days of assuming non-compromising stances and frequent protests and sit-ins probably viewed my tenure as too conciliatory and, therefore, weak. Alternatively, some regarded my focus on pragmatism, inclusiveness, and building a broader base of support for the BSA as an effective strategy given my more militant predecessors and the need to restore the BSA to a posture of perceived legitimacy at that particular time.

## GRADUATE SCHOOLS
## AND WORK SETTINGS

After graduating from UVA, I was very much a strategic thinker, a by-product of my studies and my outside of the classroom exposure. My undergraduate coursework afforded me several potential paths to graduate school. Law school seemed like a natural next step. I also had some aspiration to become a journalistic writer. In addition, I had taken courses and developed quite an interest in fitness and sports training. At the same time, I had begun working as a necessity and was accumulating experience in the counseling and helping profession.

My choice of graduate education was a master of science degree program in rehabilitation counseling. This was partially due to the fact that I was already building some quality work experience in this field on my resume. Beyond this, one of the most compelling aspects of my decision to pursue this profession was that I wanted a career path where my specific demographic profile would be rare. I did not see this as being so much the case in law, journalism, or fitness and sports training. However, when I looked around the profession of counseling and the rehabilitation professions, I saw very few graduate-degreed black men. Thus, the attribute of race influenced my choice of graduate study.

So when I entered graduate school for rehabilitation counseling, I was the only black male matriculating in the program at that time, and there were two black females. I do not recall a time in my initial graduate program when I perceived that race was a factor or that I was the victim of racism. A few years and several jobs later, I entered a doctoral program in education, and again, there were few blacks, i.e., one black female and two black males, including myself in our cohort. Again, I did not ever perceive race or racism during my tenure as a doctoral student. I do not think that higher education is devoid of racism, but there certainly is more enlightenment about racism than in other segments of society. Thus, efforts to minimize racism as a factor that motivates or influences behavior are perhaps more frequent and sustained in higher education.

My experiences in more than a half dozen work settings over thirty years have also been pretty innocuous when it comes to racism. I am not saying racism did not exist or was not a part of those settings because clearly it was, but I did not personally experience it in its covert or overt forms as far as I know. It never jumped out and hit me squarely in the face. This is significant since I had become pretty astute over the years at identifying the subtle signs of racism.

I spent the first half of my career in public mental health agencies where the mix of races in the workforce was pretty representative of the United States population as a whole, although there was a paucity of young black males who were highly educated. The second half of my career was spent in academic settings in large-majority, research-focused institutions of higher learning. In the specific settings related to my academic discipline of rehabilitation counseling, there were very few black faculty members. In my two institutional experiences in major research universities in large urban areas, my discipline was housed in schools of allied health professions or health and rehabilitation sciences along with disciplines such as physical therapy, occupational therapy, speech-language and audiology, and several others. In both institutions, I was the only tenured black faculty member. That was out of approximately 100 faculty members at each one of those universities and across nine departments in one university and seven departments in the other. Being such a rarity (or token), I was generally revered by my white faculty colleagues, and racism did not seem to be a part of those experiences as far as I could discern. Alternatively, some might argue the fact that I was the only black in those two contexts was the result of racism and that it was easy for my white colleagues to be supportive of only one black, i.e., one black faculty member in a school of over 100 faculty would not be much of a threat. What explains me being such a rarity in those settings?

I believe one plausible explanation for why I was so rare in those settings is the socialization of black professionals in health-care related disciplines. I assert that most blacks on the path to becoming a health-care professional set their sights on traditional disciplines like medicine, dentistry, nursing, and perhaps pharmacy. There are many other viable and rewarding health- and rehabilitation-related professions (e.g., occupational and physical therapy) that blacks either have not heard about or give little credence to. A common complaint among many of my fellow white allied health and health and rehabilitation science faculty professionals is that there are too few black candidates in the faculty hiring pools for these professions. To some extent this is true. However, we need to do more to creatively inform young black students during their formative years, i.e., in secondary school settings about the viability of allied health and health and rehabilitation science–related professions in order to develop a pipeline of potential faculty candidates of color. I am stopping here because this part of the discussion heads in the direction of a topic for another book.

# CULTURAL
# BIAS IS REAL

This chapter addresses the anatomy of cultural bias, making the case that it is a real, distinctly human, and natural phenomenon. I apologize in advance because this chapter may appear to be somewhat academic, but that is part of who I am. Nevertheless, I hope it illuminates some things.

America has been commonly referred to as the land of opportunity. With its faults notwithstanding and relative to other countries around the globe, this is absolutely true. The poor treatment of First Nations people (American Indians) and African Americans raises my doubt about whether America's pluralistic attribute was originally intended by its forefathers to go beyond the diversity of cultures from European countries. However, there is no doubt that today, there is a plethora of people from diverse nationalities and cultures that call America home.

The concept of pluralism means many sources of influence and authority, i.e., diverse cultural viewpoints. In the United States, a myriad of diverse cultures share this land and strive to maintain their indigenous identities. Whenever there are different cultures coexisting as they do in the United States, cultural bias is an inevitable eventuality. This is particularly the case when jockeying related to economic, political, and social power occurs. As black abolitionist Frederick Douglas said in an 1857 speech in Canandaigua, New York: "Power concedes nothing without demand. It never did and it never will." Therefore, the cultural biases of those in positions of power dominate. An important question remains: is cultural bias real?

In order to recognize that cultural bias is real, one must first have a keen understanding of cultural bias as a phenomenon. As a starting point, this discussion reviews the theoretical bases of cultural bias and the natural human processes of cognitive schemas and subjective reality that perpetuate bias. The Philosophical Aspects of Cultural Difference framework by Edwin Nichols (1989) is also discussed to make clear that diverse cultural groups have distinct and divergent worldviews. This discussion concludes outlining several strategies for overcoming the probable deleterious effects of unmanaged cultural bias when interacting across cultural lines.

Defining culture is the purview of cultural experts (i.e., anthropologists) who have posited definitions for decades, and these days many other disciplines have their ideas about culture, including sociologists, philosophers, psychologists, linguists, historians, political scientists, and others (Atkinson, 2004). Many definitions are consistent with the view of culture by Lefley (2002). Lefley contends that culture constitutes a sharing of values, beliefs, practices, and behavioral norms within a specific group of people, giving them a common identity. Pedersen (2008) maintains that the concept of cultural context includes ethnographic, demographic, status, and affiliation factors.

Beyond the formal definitions of culture, as human beings, culture is what binds us to others. Without culture, none of us would survive. Most of us have heard the cliché: "No man is an island." Well, this is true since no one lives in total isolation, at least not successfully so. Culture provides us with history, collective memory, and a way to exist now as well as go forward into the future. Culture provides a means to look back at history and see oneself as well as forward and see one's place in the future. Culture is a concept that both: brings people with a common reality together, giving them a group identity AND distinguishes those without that common reality as being outside of the group.

Because of the unique history of the United States, race and ethnicity are arguably the most prominent defining markers of culture. They continue to be sustaining features of culture because of their visible nature. Most other markers of culture are not nearly as identifiable at a glance. However, there are other markers of culture.

Cultural markers can include any dimension that speaks to a qualitative difference in worldview that binds members of a group together. Cultural groups have some aspect of worldview that is shared by its members, affording them a common group identity. Markers of culture can be race, ethnicity, language, sexual orientation, spiritual or religious orientation, social status, economic status, education level, disability status or type, age, gender, political affiliation, etc. Even with this array of cultural dimensions, race and ethnicity continue to be significant markers of cultural identity in the United States.

## THEORETICAL BASES OF BIAS

The concept of bias is often mentioned in academic literature (e.g., the counseling literature), but hardly ever is an explicit definition offered. Here are several explicit definitions. Chapman (1988) argues that bias is when one's own cultural point of view influences perception of all other individuals encountered. Biases are typically unconscious and comprised of beliefs and values that influence decision making (Gardenswartz & Rowe, 1998). A bias is the application of consistent interpretation of behavior despite differences in the cultural background of the individual (Pedersen, 2008). Bias is essentially an evaluation that is unfair (Fujiura & Drazen, 2009). Heilbronner (2011) maintains that bias is synonymous with the concepts of prejudice and partiality.

Building on the aforementioned definitions, a comprehensive working definition of cultural bias is a subconscious or conscious manifestation of one's individual cultural perspective in situations without regard for cultural differences and that can result in pejorative treatment of individuals. It is an unchecked preference for own point of view that is consciously or unconsciously expressed without regard for situations when such preference may contraindicate that which is appropriate. Given this working definition, all individuals possess cultural bias some of the time because it is virtually impossible not to apply one's own cultural point of view in some situations. In addition, at least some of the time, one is not able to adequately assess and regard cultural differences in others because cultural orientation is not always apparent. Bias when thought of as a preference is not a uniquely human phenomenon because other animals certainly have their instinctual preferences for same species. For example, with few exceptions, elephants congregate and socialize with other elephants and lions do the same with other lions as do birds and other animals when in their natural habitats.

In the human realm, basic instincts may offer partial explanatory power for the innate origin of bias. However, several theories provide assistance in understanding bias by offering social-contextual hypotheses about its derivation. The particular theoretical considerations that apply to bias are no different from the theoretical bases that address the prejudice phenomenon (Yuker, 1965; Chesler, 1965). The leading general theories to be discussed here that offer some explanatory power in understanding the etiology of bias include social learning theory, psychodynamic theory, realistic group conflict theory, social identity theory, relative deprivation theory, and ethnocentrism.

## SOCIAL LEARNING THEORY

Bandura's social learning theory (1973) maintains that bias is a learned behavior that results from observing and modeling behaviors, attitudes, and emotions of others. It is, therefore, learned in a similar manner as other attitudes through modeling, association, and reinforcement. Bias is a response to human difference that is acquired through a complex interplay of cognitive, behavioral, and environmental influences.

## PSYCHODYNAMIC THEORY

Psychodynamic theory (Adorno, Frankel-Brunswik, Levinson, & Sanford, 1950; Hahn, 1988) takes the position that bias results from motivational tension that is usually personality based. Such bias can take several forms. According to Adorno (1950), bias is more likely to be an attribute of persons with authoritarian personality syndrome, where hostility and rigidity are key features. Another form of psychodynamic based bias is displaced aggression as in the form of scapegoating toward persons who are members of marginalized groups or that have less status and perceived power. Aggression theories date back to the 1930s and 1940s and are considered to be a precursor to this theory.

## REALISTIC GROUP CONFLICT THEORY

Sherif's realistic group conflict theory (1964) argues that when groups are in competition for resources, they are at odds. Such tension creates hostility and negative evaluations between the groups, inevitably resulting in bias that does not necessarily dissipate even if the conflict over resources is resolved. The resulting bias seems to be more deep rooted and resistant to change. This theory portrays bias as an enduring phenomenon that can be sustained even when the precipitating conditions are eliminated.

## SOCIAL IDENTITY THEORY

Social identity or minimal group theory maintains that bias starts with the mere knowing that another group exists (Turner & Tajfel, 1979). According to Turner and Tajfel, this urge is so compelling that it exists in situations where groups are formed of complete strangers and told of a fictitious group. At that point, derogatory attitudes toward the unknown group and favoritism toward one's own group increase.

## RELATIVE DEPRIVATION THEORY

Relative deprivation theory contends that bias results from in-group perceptions when the group perceives that it has less access to power, resources, and opportunity than does another group (Walker & Smith, 2002). This is a perceptual phenomenon that creates intergroup rivalry that leads to bias despite any actual status disparities or lack thereof.

## ETHNOCENTRISM

Sumner defined ethnocentrism (1960) as viewing the perspectives of one's own group as the standard against which all other groups must be measured and, therefore, maintaining (subconsciously or consciously) that all other groups are inherently inferior. This view of believing that one's own group is superior to all others intellectually, psychologically, and physically when taken to the extreme is the beginning attribute of racism (Atkinson, Morten, & Sue, 1998). As a term, racism applies to the superiority-inferiority dynamic in situations where race is the defining cultural marker, and in a more general sense, the term *racism* is considered synonymous with the term *ethnocentrism* and, in such cases, merely refers to non–race-based cultural differences (Atkinson, Morten, & Sue,

1998). Such differences might include ethnicity and national origin, gender, sexual orientation, religion, and disability.

Ethnocentrism in its more extreme form, as racism, typically leads to prejudicial attitudes or bias. Prejudice includes negative thoughts, beliefs, and attitudes toward an entire group (Schaffer, 1988). Prejudice, when manifested behaviorally, can take the form of racist acts. Racist acts involve discriminatory behavior that can take on subtle forms (Van Dijk, 1993) as in covert manifestations or can be more overt and often violent in form (Atkinson, Morten, & Sue, 1998).

The previous discussion offers several theoretical viewpoints that provide hypotheses on the origin of cultural bias. Cultural bias is certainly a factor in many situations. Given this, it makes sense to attempt to understand the natural human processes that perpetuate bias.

## NATURAL HUMAN PROCESSES THAT PERPETUATE BIAS

Human beings are naturally programmed to be biased. This is a logical conclusion given the several definitions of bias presented earlier in this discussion, and this point will become even clearer after the upcoming discussion of cognitive schemas and subjective reality. Realizing this natural human propensity toward bias removes the tendency toward indictment of the human species for this normal and typically helpful attribute. Humans make sense of difference in a manner that is systematic and that promotes a sense of efficiency in order to manage the many and vast differences in the world. The two main processes that humans rely on are cognitive schemas and subjective reality.

Cognitive schemas are mental frameworks in the brain designed to sort and classify the physical realities of the human experience (Piaget, 1972). They are unconscious structures that the brain develops that represent the world (Huntington,

1999). When an individual is presented with a new physical stimulus (i.e., an object never before encountered), the brain develops a preliminary category based on the perceivable physical characteristics of that stimulus (i.e., the object). As the individual encounters more of this same object, the brain develops a set of key attributes that classify this object. Then, a cognitive category or schema exists in the brain, and with each new encounter of that same object, the individual then knows how to classify it, and over time, the schema gains permanence.

Even when the individual encounters an object that has some but not all of the key physical attributes, the brain is still likely to classify it the same way (Huntington, 1999). This process is called assimilation and is one of Piaget's functional invariants (1972), meaning it occurs the same way in all humans. If an individual is exposed to a new object, then the functional invariant process of accommodation occurs to either create a new schema or to expand the pool of attributes that constitute the defining elements of the original schema. Together, the processes of assimilation and accommodation are somewhat balanced in most individuals and this balance is called equilibration, another functional invariant (Piaget, 1972).

Cognitive schemas are a contributing factor in the development of stereotypes because humans tend to be somewhat subjective and modify reality to fit existing cognitive structures (Cherry, 2011). Also, the brain in its quest for efficiency is more likely to assimilate new reality (i.e., experiences) into an existing schema, allowing previous experience to prevail, then it is to accommodate and change the schema or develop a new one (Cherry, 2011). Therefore, the tendency for prior experience to override new reality contributes to the development of stereotypes at the level of cognitive schemas in the human brain.

# We are All Racists:
## the Truth about Cultural Bias

Stereotypes are overgeneralizations about groups (Atkinson, Morten, & Sue, 1998). There is disagreement on what mechanism of action undergirds human beings' proclivity to stereotype. Some maintain that prejudice perpetuates stereotypes (e.g., Schaffer, 1988), which implies some culpability of the individual who holds them. The view that the formation of stereotypes is not a culpable activity and is merely a natural by-product of Piaget's cognitive schema mechanism as we attempt to manage a world of cognitive overload is supported by others (e.g., Brown, 1965). The schema hypothesis seems most plausible as to why stereotypes form initially, and then later, the role of prejudice could be an augmenting factor.

It seems that every stereotype has basis in reality in that clearly there are some individuals in the group to which the stereotype applies that possess the attribute that is the essence of the stereotype. The problem surfaces when everyone in the group is considered to have the stereotyped attribute. Consider this example. There are clearly some Asian Americans who have advanced math skills. This is absolutely true. The issue is that humans, due to the cognitive schema mechanism, tend to overgeneralize erroneously what is true for a small sample of individuals to an entire group of individuals. Not every Asian American has advanced math skills. So essentially, stereotypes are based in reality in that some individuals in the group exhibit the attribute, but the stereotype fails when what is true for a small sample is generalized to an entire population of individuals. It is as simple as the statistical dilemma of the sample not being adequately representative of the entire population.

Stereotypes and cognitive schemas are natural human processes and so is subjective reality. Subjective reality is the total of an individual's experiences (i.e., it is reality through an individual's eyes). It is based on life experience. Subjective reality has to do with how past experiences help to interpret, understand, and lend meaning to the present.

Cognitive schemas and subjective reality are both uniquely human, but different. On the one hand, cognitive schemas help humans to identify reality based primarily on the physical attributes of that reality. Alternatively, subjective reality helps to apply broad meaning to the reality once it is identified. Both are based on individual experiences. Here is an example that may illuminate the distinction between these two critically important concepts. If one were to hold up a Confederate flag in a college classroom almost anywhere in the United States, most students would be able to identify the object as the Confederate flag. This is because in United States society, there is some commonality of cognitive schemas across persons relative to the physical attributes of flags in general and the specific characteristics of the Confederate flag. If each student in that same college classroom was then asked to describe the meaning of the Confederate flag, there would be divergent viewpoints. This is because the subjective reality of what the Confederate flag symbolizes and stands for would be different among the students based on cultural orientation (e.g., race) and life experience.

Another example would be if one were to hold up a photograph of a wheelchair in a college classroom anywhere in the United States. Most students would correctly identify it for what it is due to societal consensus on the specific physical attributes that comprise a wheelchair. There would be a common perspective on what constitutes a wheelchair (i.e., the wheelchair schema). However, if students were asked to describe what the wheelchair means for them, there would be varied perspectives. For some individuals without mobility impairments, a photograph of a wheelchair might symbolize confinement or something negative. However, for a student with a disability and mobility functional limitation (e.g., a person with a spinal cord injury), a wheelchair may represent independence and freedom to move about because perhaps without such a device, mobility would be more challenging. Again, individualized life experiences influence one's subjective reality and the meaning attached to objects and situations.

Together, cognitive schemas and subjective reality work to create stereotypes. Consider this overly simplistic example. If a white individual encounters a black individual for the first time, before they interact, the white person will see (perceive) the black person. (This is normally a two-way/reciprocal process, but for brevity of this example, only one direction is used.) Based on the white person's cognitive schema for blacks (e.g., dark skin, broad facial features, and dark hair), the white individual will identify this individual as black. (For this illustration, it is assumed that the individual actually is black.) Depending on the white person's predominant subjective reality about blacks (i.e., total of past experiences interfacing with blacks) conforms to a "drug dealer" versus a "productive citizen" model of blacks will determine the white person's perspective (i.e., stereotype) about this particular new black individual just met. In other words, the white individual will align this new black person just met with either a drug dealer or productive citizen stereotype. When stereotypes are perpetuated over time, they help to generate and crystallize cultural bias. Stereotypes have context and meaning based on particular worldviews.

## CULTURAL GROUPS HAVE DIFFERENT WORLDVIEWS

According to Dr. Edwin Nichols and his framework "The Philosophical Aspects of Cultural Difference," that dates back to 1976 in its earliest iteration and 1987 in its latest, different cultural groups experience the world in different ways (i.e., have different worldviews), using standard philosophical processes (1989). This framework sorts cultures into four groups thought to be homogeneous in terms of worldview: (1) European and

European American; (2) African American, African, Latino, and Arab; (3) Asian, Asian American, Polynesian, and individuals from India; and (4) Native Americans. Next, the differences in worldview are illustrated across the philosophical dimensions of axiology (that which has value), logic (principles of reasoning), process (the practice of reasoning), and epistemology (ways of knowing).

Epistemology is divided into the following three components according to Nichols (1989). Applied epistemology is concerned with how we come to know or the practice of knowing (i.e., the basis of knowledge). Applied epistemology also relates to exploring if approaches for seeking knowledge are adequate and sufficient to lead to truth (Laudan, 2006). Pedagogical epistemology speaks to approaches for teaching methodology. Methodological epistemology addresses the formal approaches and rules used for inquiry and analysis within a discipline (e.g., social research).

For illustration purposes only, here is a brief paraphrased overview of what Nichols maintains is the European and European-American worldview (i.e., the Western perspective) from his framework when it comes to several of the philosophical aspects. In terms of axiology, in Western culture, the emphasis is on the acquisition of objects by its group members (i.e., materialism). Applied epistemology or how we come to know or the practice of knowing is based on counting or measuring, as in empiricism from the Western point of view. The pedagogical or teaching process related to methodology is inductive in that the focus is on exposure to the constituent parts first and, subsequently, how they comprise the whole. Methodologically speaking, epistemology addresses the formal approaches and rules for inquiry and analysis within a discipline that are based on linear and sequential models in the European and European-American traditions. The basis of logic (principles of reasoning) is dichotomous thinking (i.e., an either/or thought process). Process (the practice of reasoning) is based primarily on replication and a strong inclination toward technology.

Nichols's contention about distinct and divergent worldviews is not an anomaly. Other writers have provided support for his viewpoint either in general or with respect to specific components. For example, Addison (2009) supports Nichols's approach in general and specifically references the points about axiology in his book that analyzes racism and slavery in America. In another example, Pedersen (1987) provides support for Nichols's view by stating that within the realm of Western counseling there is an inherent assumption about linear and cause-effect thinking that is integral to the European and European-American/Western perspective on methodology. Usher (1989), in a discussion of counseling, talks about cause-effect thinking and measuring concepts and then contrasts this Western approach with the African circular approach where causes and effects may be more blended and comprise a singular continuous thought process.

The fact that there is an ongoing debate in the discipline of the philosophy of science around epistemology and methodology also provides a measure of support for the Nichols's way of thinking. In that debate, epistemology is framed as being more concerned with determining what knowledge is possible and its adequacy (Maynard & Purvis, 2002); methodology is more practically inclined and focuses on the practice of generating knowledge (Trochim, 2006). Furthermore, with respect to methodology, the discussion of the approaches of scientific inquiry ranges from the positivist perspective (science is that which can be measured or observed using maximum objectivity) (Trochim, 2006), to the post-positivist perspective (scientific thinking is comparative, and this includes experimental and causal approaches) (Fujiura & Drazen, 2009), to the constructivist perspective (science can legitimately include subjectivity) (Fujiura & Drazen, 2009), to the transformative tradition (science can include historical, social, and cultural factors) (Fujiura & Drazen, 2009).

## MANAGING BIAS: A SELF-EVALUATION PROCESS

Differences in worldview, as previously discussed, provide the context within which cultural bias can contraindicate individuals interacting successfully across cultural lines. Therefore, a process is needed to manage cultural bias. In order to manage bias and mitigate its potential negative effects, it behooves individuals to be proactive. The following self-evaluation process is intended to be a guide in doing just that. To effectively identify cultural bias requires an active and candid introspective search in which one takes an inventory of those issues that could decrease effectiveness when interacting with individuals of a specific cultural orientation. While the purpose of the self-evaluation process is to identify issues that may pose a barrier to effective cross-cultural interactions, the process is intended to elicit all personal biases since it is difficult to know which biases might surface at a given time. Additionally, the self-evaluation process is not intended to be overly prescriptive, although there is some benefit to embarking on this exploration using a systematic approach, applying the four steps below to each personal bias separately. Note: that a statement with a sample bias is included in italics at the end of each of the four steps for illustration purposes only.

### STEP 1: UNDERSTAND THE TRUE NATURE OF THE BIAS

Identify and describe the bias in clear terms. Acknowledge how long you have been aware of the bias. Provide a personal hypothesis on why this is a bias for you. Determine the extent to which this bias is permanent or amenable to change. If the bias can be changed, try to identify what will modify it (e.g., education, exposure, etc.). If the bias is not prone to change, begin thinking about management strategies.

*The sample bias is a deep-rooted disdain for visible racial and ethnic minorities held by a white person. The hypothesized reason for the existence of this bias is that in my experience, minorities are always looking for a handout, case in point affirmative action. I have actually lost out on opportunities to lesser qualified minorities due to affirmative action. I believe this bias could be amenable to change with increased education and understanding of the challenges faced by minority populations in the United States.*

## STEP 2: UNDERSTAND THE POTENTIAL NEGATIVE IMPACT OF THE BIAS

Evaluate how this bias specifically impacts you. Consider how it could compromise your interactions with others. Acknowledge the type of person that may invoke this bias. Identify specifically how this bias might negatively impact the individuals with whom you interact.

*This bias renders me less than effective in my personal interactions with a large proportion of individuals. It could damage the relationships I have with culturally diverse individuals that comprise the US population. Anyone who is a visible racial or ethnic minority (African American, Latino American, Asian American, or American Indian) might invoke this bias. This bias will not allow me to interact effectively with individuals from culturally diverse backgrounds.*

## STEP 3: IDENTIFY STRATEGIES FOR SUCCESSFULLY MANAGING THE BIAS

Determine how you will mitigate the potential negative impact of the bias on you and, more importantly, the persons with whom you routinely interact. Decide how you will proactively monitor the potential negative impact of the bias on you and those you encounter in an ongoing manner. Identify how you will pilot test the management strategies in a manner that is low risk. Develop a plan and time frame for updating the management strategies going forward.

*I will try to mitigate this bias since I think it is amenable to change by engaging in self-study to learn more facts about the ethnic/racial minority experience in the United States and by joining a black church to develop some friendships and hopefully insights about this particular cultural group. For my plan, I will begin the self-study process and join the new church immediately.*

## STEP 4: REALIZE THE PERSONAL LEARNING THE BIAS PROVIDES

Identify the lesson(s) you have learned about who you are as an individual as a result of having the bias (e.g., personal fallibility, need for lifelong learning/continuous quality improvement, etc.). List the implications of the lesson(s) you have learned from identifying this bias for your overall lifetime. Develop a plan to revisit this four-step process routinely over the course of one's life.

*One major lesson that I have learned from identifying this bias is that even though I have lots of great qualities, I am not perfect and still have my challenges. I must commit to overcoming this specific challenge now, but more importantly, I must always be vigilant to other biases that I have that are to date unidentified or that may evolve over time as I grow and change as a human being. Identifying biases is a lifelong process. I must always stay on top of my current bias, any others that I may develop later, and be constantly engaging in self-reflection and evaluation for new biases for the duration of my life.*

This four-step process just described is by no means a panacea. However, it is an intentional, stepwise approach for beginning to identify, understand, and manage cultural bias. With practice, this process could become a habit that not only leads to to more effective management of cultural bias, but ideally should mitigate its potential negative impact in interpersonal situations with individuals who are culturally diverse.

## DISMANTLING DYSFUNCTIONAL COGNITIVE SCHEMAS

Some cognitive schemas are dysfunctional and need to be dismantled. In order to do this, it is necessary to understand cognitive schema development from the perspectives of inductive and deductive reasoning. This will have the benefit of illustrating how a self-aware individual can interrupt, dismantle, and correct dysfunctional cognitive schemas. The purpose is to provide individuals with a way to consciously override the perpetuation of counterproductive schemas to have more effective interactions with others.

In reviewing table 2, which lays out the dismantling process, it is important to realize that most individuals function continuously in stages 1 through 3 in autopilot mode. An initial schema is formed; it then becomes confirmed by another similar experience or two. At this point, the schema is essentially locked in, crystallized as a stereotype until a profound experience forces schema modification or change. This is mostly a subconscious process. However, the optimum scenario is that through self-awareness and conscious effort, individuals can do better by forcing the cognitive schema process to routinely include stages 4 and 5. This ensures that inductive reasoning prevails over deductive reasoning. Deductive reasoning allows past experience to prevail, while inductive reasoning allows the specifics in a given situation to influence judgments, and the latter is preferred.

When individuals force themselves to see each situation anew, inductive reasoning predominates. It is when deductive reasoning prevails that stereotypes begin to form because only then is there a propensity to attempt to fit all new encounters into an existing schema. The bottom line is that individuals attempting to be culturally sensitive would prefer to produce a new or modified schema with each new acquaintance. This way, the functional invariant process of accommodation occurs more than assimilation. Accommodation equates to the formation of new schemas for new individuals, enhancing the probability for appropriate and positive interactions among culturally different individuals. Essentially, accommodation offers the best opportunity to view and understand an individual's unique attributes.

# We are All Racists:
## the Truth about Cultural Bias

Table 1: *Interrupting Dysfunctional Cognitive Schemas*

| Stage | Instrumental Mental Process |
|---|---|
| 1) Individual has an experience for the first time. A preliminary cognitive pattern develops. | **Inductive Reasoning** moving from the specific to the general, i.e., taking a specific experience and allowing it to begin establishing a general cognitive pattern to be applied broadly in the future. |
| 2) Individual has a further experience or two similar to the initial experience, and the brain crystallizes a general pattern (schema) of the thing/experience, which indicates that all such things or experiences within a certain range of specific attributes are to be categorized in the same manner. | **Inductive Reasoning** to confirm the formation of the initial cognitive pattern and **Deductive Reasoning** as applied to future exposures. |
| 3) Individual encounters a specific thing or experience with some, but perhaps not all attributes similar to the existing schema, and the brain categorizes this new encounter and future individual encounters according to the pre-existing schema (assimilation functional invariant process). | **Deductive Reasoning** moving from the general to the specific, i.e., taking a broad rule that was originally formulated based on a specific experience or two, but now applying it broadly to all such specific situations with a similar range of attributes. |
| 4) In a specific interpersonal situation, one individual encounters another individual who does **not** fit nicely into a pre-existing schema, so the pattern does not hold. | **Forced Inductive Reasoning** to modify the schema, allowing the unique attributes presented by this individual to be validated. |
| 5) Individual modifies existing schema to reflect new individual encountered. The new or modified schema is based on new data, and becomes a static categorization until the next situation violates it, making modification necessary (accommodation functional invariant process). | **Forced Inductive Reasoning** for schema modification, but then **Deductive Reasoning** in future encounters until modification is warranted again. |

With an understanding of this process above, the individual who is self-aware and culturally versatile can be sure that s/he does not function on autopilot, allowing those natural human processes to play out unmonitored and result in inappropriate perceptions and conclusions. Such inappropriate perceptions would only serve to catalyze the human inclination toward cultural bias and provide a disservice to individuals encountered from culturally diverse backgrounds.

This chapter makes clear that all of us as humans are guilty of cultural bias. While the form that bias takes can differ in that some of us will possess biases related to race, ethnicity, spirituality, gender, age, sexual orientation, political affiliation, education, social class, social economic status, etc., we each have bias of some sort. Our distinctive humanness along with the cognitive and experience based processes render us inclined toward cultural bias, which if goes unchecked can be a precursor to extreme forms of bias, e.g., ethnocentricity taken to an extreme or racism. No one is immune and so the problem is not us or them, but every one of us. We are all racists!

# WHAT THE PAST TELLS US

## BLACK ADVANCEMENT/WHITE BACKLASH

When I was an undergraduate student at UVA, one of the requirements in my major in African-American and African Studies was to complete a senior thesis. Since I had two majors, the other one being Rhetoric and Communication Studies, my personal goal was to complete the senior thesis requirement in a manner that allowed me to integrate my learning in both majors. Pursuant to this goal, I decided to examine two periods in history, one in the nineteenth century and the other in the twentieth century, which had some parallels.

As a student of African-American history, I was keenly aware of the political strides made by blacks in the South immediately following the Civil War. I was familiar with black accomplishments beyond the common knowledge of many individuals who generally knew about the promise of "40 acres and a mule" and the existence of the Freedmen's Bureau, both designed to help newly freed blacks. For example, I had heard of Hiram Revels, the first black elected to the United States Senate in the 1860s, who occupied the seat vacated by Jefferson

Davis. I had also heard of Blanche Bruce who was elected to the United States Senate from the state of Mississippi in 1875. My background in black history meant I was well acquainted with the fact that there were more than a dozen blacks serving in the United States Congress, along with several hundred black representatives serving in elected positions in state legislatures and localities in the South during the Reconstruction era. The Fifteenth Amendment that was passed in 1869 afforded black men the right to vote. The first Civil Rights Act was passed in 1875, giving blacks equal protection in transportation, restaurants, theaters, hotels, and on juror duty.

I recognized that these post–Civil War gains made by blacks were short-lived as a movement of white backlash ensued to terminate this progress. Beginning in 1883, the white backlash began with the weakening of the Civil Rights Act of 1875 when the courts ruled that the Act only prohibited government discrimination and not discrimination perpetrated by private parties or entities. In 1896, the *Plessy v. Ferguson* United States Supreme Court decision confirmed states' rights to establish separate, but equal facilities that ushered in segregation. By 1900, the Ku Klux Klan had hit its stride with killings and had lynched an estimated several thousand blacks, primarily in the South.

I was aware of the second period in United States history where blacks had made substantial political and social gains only to have them begin to be dismantled by white backlash. That period of advancement was almost a century later with the beginning of the Civil Rights era. The Civil Rights era began with the passage of the Brown decision in 1954 that struck down segregation and commenced the Civil Rights movement. In the next decade, additional legislation was passed as in the Civil Rights Act of 1964 and the Voting Rights Act of 1965. The time between the Brown decision and the passage of the 1964 and 1965 legislation under the leadership of President

Lyndon B. Johnson along with the advocacy of black leaders like Dr. Martin Luther King, Jr. and El-Hajj Malik El-Shabazz (Malcolm X) marked a period of black advancement in this country. Some, like black scholar Lerone Bennett, Jr., in his 1962 book *Before the Mayflower*, have termed that period of black advancement the Second Reconstruction. However, that period of black advancement was not to continue.

As was the case with the first Reconstruction period, the Civil Rights era was halted by a period of white backlash. This second white backlash period commenced with the 1978 Bakke Supreme Court decision that began to weaken affirmative action. Subsequently, President Ronald Reagan was elected in 1980. His two terms saw the resurgence of modern conservatism as well as new federalism and states' rights, a political configuration wherein states exercise maximum autonomy, refusing federal government intervention at will. It is under the states' rights model of government that injustices like slavery and segregation flourished.

Remembering these two periods in American history almost a century apart, where blacks had initially been given help only to lose it when white support of black progress declined, I was intrigued by these cycles of growth and retrenchment and wanted to study them. However, I wanted to study them in a nontraditional manner and incorporate my Rhetoric and Communication Studies major. Then, I had an epiphany! I would examine the public sentiment during these two cycles (four time periods) in both the black and white communities and compare them. The time periods were: First Reconstruction/ blacks advanced (1865–1882), First White Backlash (1883– 1953), Second Reconstruction/blacks advanced (1954–1977), and Second White Backlash (1978–1983). Actually, I was doing my senior thesis in 1983, so the time period for the Second White Backlash had to end there. However, had I been doing it now, I probably would have extended the end date for the Second White Backlash period up through the presidency of George H. W. Bush (January 20, 1993).

My angle was to do a rhetorical analysis, which is an evaluation of a persuasive situation: the demands within a social, political, or economic context and how well a discourse or argument responds to such demands. In conducting this rhetorical analysis, I assessed the types and structures of the arguments made in the white and black communities as reflected in public discourses, i.e., editorials in black and white newspapers (black papers: *Richmond Planet* and *Richmond Afro-American*, white papers: *Richmond Times Dispatch* and *Richmond Newsleader*). My goal was to compare the lay attitudes of blacks versus whites as reflected in published editorials in the periods of black advancement and white backlash in the nineteenth and twentieth centuries.

Because of my major in Rhetoric and Communication Studies, I was well equipped and quite facile at critiquing written discourse. The framework I used to critique the editorials in four newspapers was based on these seven elements: (1) the subject matter, i.e., whether it addressed a racial issue, (2) the exigencies and constraints of the topic, i.e., did the discourse maintain due diligence in addressing things that the topic/occasion required to be addressed and in avoiding things that were not proper to be addressed, respectively, (3) author's stated versus implicit purpose, (4) use of language, (5) type and strength of argument(s) and evidence, (6) conclusion, and (7) my assessment of the overall attitude reflected by the author based on previous elements 1–6.

In all, I reviewed forty editorials. I randomly selected five editorials each from the black and white newspapers during the First Reconstruction period and five editorials each from the black and white newspapers during the First White Backlash period. Next, I randomly selected five editorials each from the black and white newspapers during the Second Reconstruction period and five editorials each from the black and white newspapers during the Second White Backlash period.

My findings indicated several patterns in terms of attitudes. First, the attitudes of blacks in both Reconstruction periods overwhelmingly reflected enthusiasm and optimism for the positive possibilities that both periods promised and had begun to demonstrate for improving the black condition in this country. Somewhat similarly, there were attitudes of guarded hope and cautious or tentative optimism for black advancement among whites early on during these periods of advancement. During the periods of white backlash, the attitudes among blacks reflected shock, disappointment, and betrayal that the momentum toward a better day and life were in jeopardy with the resurgence of the old white attitudes that were all too familiar. Attitudes among whites during these backlash periods were of resentment and bitterness that blacks had contemplated for even a brief moment being on even footing with whites. During the Second White Backlash period, there was a definitive attitude of being threatened by blacks and efforts to give them a helping hand through social interventions like affirmative action.

Essentially, the within and between racial group parallels in attitudes across the considerable time span were eerily similar. It was as if history really did repeat itself. Is history continuing to repeat itself? This is one among several other important questions now.

Are these periods of advancement and backlash/retrenchment still happening? Did we have another period of advancement for blacks and other minorities during the Bill Clinton Presidencies? Were the two presidencies of George W. Bush a period of white backlash? Are the two presidencies of Barack Obama yet another period of black/minority advancement? Is the Republican/Tea Party conservative reaction and opposition to President Obama the beginnings of another period of white backlash, including the Supreme Court's 2013 ruling that nullified key aspects of the 1965 Voting Rights legislation? These are interesting questions. You be the judge.

## RACISM AGAINST OTHER MINORITY GROUPS

In reading the previous section, one might arrive at the conclusion that blacks have been the only disenfranchised group in America identified by race or ethnicity. Though no other group in America has endured the oppression of chattel slavery, clearly other minority groups have been victims of racism. First Nations Americans, Chinese Americans, Japanese Americans, Mexican Americans, and Arab Americans have all been victims of systematic societal racism American style. I want to apologize to these aforementioned groups that my representation of their victimization by America will not be a full account, but will only comprise a few examples of the racism they have endured for brief illustrative purposes.

First Nations Americans were robbed of their land from the moment the first European settlers landed in North America in the early 1600s. The oppression was continuous and included the massacre of hundreds of innocent men, women, and children by the United States military at the battle of Wounded Knee in 1890; being relegated to reservations; and other oppressive acts that have not relented today. Chinese Americans were required to carry special identification cards and had their immigration patterns restricted for a period of twenty years by the Chinese Exclusion Acts of 1882 and 1892. Back then, Chinese Americans were only allowed into the United States as laborers. In 1912, the Mexican ambassador to America protested numerous murders and lynchings of innocent Mexican Americans. Over 100,000 Japanese Americans were committed to internment or relocation camps at the conclusion of WWII due to American paranoia. Guards were ordered to fire at anyone attempting to leave those camps. Arab Americans are routinely targeted as suspects in any terrorist act committed against the United States, and especially since the attacks on the World Trade Centers on September 11, 2001.

The bottom line is that there have been many victims of oppression in America. Those victims have typically been members of groups identified based on race or ethnicity. Again, visible difference has played a significant role. The need for healing in the targeted communities is clear.

# HEALING IN COMMUNITIES: BLACK COMMUNITY EXEMPLAR

It should be clear based on the discussion so far that all of the racial/ethnic minority communities in this country have some healing to do as a result of having been victims of racism historically. The healing process for each community is something that only those specific communities can speak to in terms of what needs to be done to facilitate wellness. To speak for those communities would be paternalistic. All community healing strategies must be self-determined.

There is probably no one who can speak for an entire community. Nevertheless, my charge in this chapter is to provide some ideas, my own, about what the healing is that needs to occur within the black community. After all, I have lived the experience of having been a member of this community for more than 50 years. My hope is that this could provide an exemplar of the types of strategies that might be considered by other racial/ethnic minority communities in need of healing.

The discussion of the black community will include several subtopics. First, I will provide an empirical picture of the current status of the black condition in America. In so doing, I will present data on several key indices. I call these data points "indices of oppression in the black community." Each data point will be compared to data from the majority white culture. This assumes that the goal is for minority communities to exhibit comparable patterns to that of the majority community. Historically, this type of side-by-side comparison has been made without much questioning of this assumption that the groups should be comparable. So for the record and before making such direct comparisons, I think it is prudent to acknowledge an alternative point of view that perhaps the only true and fair comparison is to one's own standards within a group.

Secondly, I will address the current psyche of the black community. To do this, I will address the pervasive culture of narcissism that exists today. There is also a false sense that everything is fine that exists in some segments of the black community that I will discuss. I cannot avoid addressing the spending patterns of the black community and the lack of entrepreneurs and wealth generation. Additionally, I will discuss the lack of viable and sustainable black leadership.

Next, I will discuss the presidency of Barack Obama. Primarily, this will entail coverage of the attempts to sabotage his success and a few contemporary issues, such as how the fervor around the purchase of guns and protection of the Second Amendment may be a form of white backlash against Obama's presidency. There are some other recent occurrences that may also be manifestations of white backlash that will be mentioned.

Following the discussion of the opposition to President Obama, I will provide a few personal observations that I believe speak to the magnitude of the challenge of improving the black condition in America. I also have some thoughts about why black male role modeling has not been as successful as it should have been to date. There is a key link that I believe black males are missing in effective role modeling. The final segment of this chapter will outline ten common-sense self-help strategies to elevate the black community.

## CURRENT STATUS OF THE BLACK CONDITION: A DATA PERSPECTIVE

If there is anyone out there who truly believes that blacks and whites in 2014 have achieved a level of parity in that the quality of their respective American experiences is comparable, think again. I endeavored to take a quick empirical glance (i.e., data-driven perspective) at where things stand on eleven key indices. These "indices of oppression in the black community" are (in no particular order) life expectancy, poverty rate, homelessness rate, unemployment rate, high school drop-out rate, four-year high school graduation rate, college graduation rate, teenage pregnancy rate, incidence rate of selected diseases (cancer and diabetes), mortality rate of selected diseases (cancer), and the incarceration rate. Please review all of the numbers in the table below closely. There are a few noteworthy comparisons where the disparities are most prominent such as the poverty rate, homelessness rate, unemployment rate, high school and college graduation rates, teenage pregnancy rate, and incarceration rate. Please keep in mind when making comparisons that the black population is 13 percent of the entire United States population.

Of course, I could have selected other indices upon which to make comparisons, but I believe these provide a complete and balanced picture. I am certain the trends would have been the same no matter which specific data dimensions I could have included. For example, think about what we all know about the black versus white incidence and mortality rates for other selected diseases such as morbid obesity, hypertension, stroke, heart disease, and communicable diseases like AIDS?

Table 2: *A Data Perspective on the Black Community in the U. S. Using Eleven Key Indices*

| Indices | Black | White |
|---|---|---|
| Life expectancy | 73.7 years | 78.4 years (2008 – National Center for Health Statistics) |
| Poverty rate | 35% | 13% (2011- Kaiser Family Foundation) |
| Homelessness rate | Black families are **seven times** more likely to end up in a shelter than white families (2012 - Institute for Child Poverty and Homelessness) | |
| Unemployment rate | 14.3% | 6.8% (June 2013 - U.S. Bureau of Labor Statistics) |
| High school drop-out rate | 8% | 5.1% (2010 - National Center of Education Statistics) |
| Four-year high school graduation rate | 52% | 78% (2006-07 year - Schott Foundation for Public Education) |
| College graduation rate (first generation college enrollees, 6-year graduation rate for full-time students) | 39% (on the upswing) | 62% (2010 - National Center of Education Statistics) |
| Teenage pregnancy rate | 47 births/1000 | 22 births/1000 (Centers for Disease Control data over five years: 2007-11 for 15-19 year olds, rate is per 1000) |
| Incidence rate of selected diseases- | | |
| Cancer: | 480.2 cases/100,000 | 466 cases/100,000 (2005 -National Cancer Institute) |
| Diabetes: | 12.6% | 7.1% (National Health Interview Survey data from 2007-09 and adjusted for population, includes only persons 20+ years old) |
| Mortality rate of selected diseases (Cancer) | 224.1 cases/100,000 | 182.7 cases/100,000 (2005 - National Cancer Institute) |
| Incarceration rate (state prisons only) | 52% (Black male rate has dropped 10% from 2000-2009 and female rate dropped 31% in same 10 yrs. Black males are still 6+ **times** more likely to be jailed than white males.) | 48% (2011 – U.S. Bureau of Justice Statistics) |

# THE PSYCHE OF THE BLACK COMMUNITY

Christopher Lasch's 1979 bestselling book, *Culture of Narcissism: American Life in an Age of Diminishing Expectations*, makes clear that Americans now (thirty-five years ago when Lasch's book was written) are experiencing a decline in the importance of family, there is more emphasis on self and greater feelings of entitlement. In 2014, it seems this culture of narcissism has reached unparalleled heights in the black community. By and large, blacks have adopted an "I've got mine, now you get yours" mentality. Never before has the metaphor of "crabs in the bucket" been so applicable. Anyone familiar with crabs knows a group of crabs in a bucket will not allow any single crab to climb out. The typical behavior is that those on the bottom will pull down any crab that attempts to escape the bucket. This is characteristic of the behavior of some blacks apparently believing and behaving as if there is limited room in the circle of success. Ostensibly, there is plenty of room for us all to be successful and achieve that proverbial American dream. That is, unless we bring into the discussion that capitalism as an economic model may by definition force there to be an upper, middle, and lower class, offering limited room in each class. Let's not go there. That is an entirely different discussion.

As a result of this culture of narcissism that seems to have gripped the black community, rarely do we work collectively toward anything, except for the election of Barack Obama, being outraged about the George Zimmerman verdict, and a few other isolated instances where black community collectivism has been shown to have reached elevated heights. Part of what accounts for this pervasive mentality of "me-ism" is that in 2014, there are several decoys that support the perception that we have all arrived in Utopia. For example, there are fewer overt manifestations of racism. There are some, but relatively few in the grand scheme of things. There are highly visible black millionaires—mostly athletes and entertainers, and we have a black president, or at least one that looks black. Therefore, it is easy for the non-discerning black person to arrive at the conclusion that everything must be okay today. I believe this perception is more common than many want to admit. Let's face it, we now have a generation of young adults, the Generation Millennials, who were not alive during the Civil

Rights movement and who believe that those struggles are now ancient history.

Blacks also have challenges when it comes to money and spending. Let's be clear that the assumption I am operating under is that there should be parity across the racial/ethnic groups. Again, some may question this assumption asserting that performance by blacks on any dimension should be an intra-race comparison, i.e., a comparison within our own group only. You may have heard the argument that black achievement and pride was never higher than when there were separate black and white institutions pre-integration, and that integration has resulted in a dulling of black prominence and success. This is a good point that I once made myself some years ago in a paper for a doctoral course on educational history. Nevertheless, I submit that we do make these interracial comparisons all the time and have made them for years, so I am going with it for now.

The buying power of blacks in the United States is projected to reach one trillion dollars by 2015, according to a 2012 Nielson study. To put this into perspective, blacks make up about 13 percent of the nation's population, but that rate of spending outpaces the remaining 87 percent of the population by 30 percent. If this is not staggering enough, a recent report from the Urban Institute that examined 2010 data said that on average white families have twice the total income of black families and this pattern has been the same for the past thirty years. Moreover, the black-white disparity is really apparent in terms of wealth, where white families have on average six times the wealth as black families.

For those who think that blacks have closed the gap in terms of entrepreneurship and business ownership, think again. Constituting 13 percent of the population, blacks own 5 percent of businesses in the nation, and most of those are single employee operations (i.e., the owner is the only employee) with blacks owning less than 2 percent of businesses that have more than one employee according to a 2007 United States Small Business Administration (SBA) report on minority owned businesses. According to that same SBA report, black-owned companies earned 43 cents, compared to 56 cents made by Asian, First Nations, and Latino-American firms, and 59 cents made by firms owned by Pacific Island Americans on each dollar that white owned firms earned. To further add insult to injury, it is expected that the Sequestration cuts will have a disproportionately negative impact on black-owned businesses because they depend more on government contracts than other majority owned businesses according to a 2012 Gazelle Index report.

Since most visible vestiges of systemic and overt racism and discrimination have disappeared from the vantage point of the casual/non-discerning observer, it may appear as if there is no need for viable and sustainable leadership like Martin, Malcolm, and Mandela of the previous two generations. Yes, we do have the cadre of Al Sharpton, Jesse Jackson, Cornell West, and a few others who are very willing to speak out and take stands episodically, and I give each one of them their deserved respect, but it appears as if there is no need for a viable and sustained black leadership presence these days. I submit this is probably a deception or misinterpretation of reality because overt racism is still alive and well (evidence: in 2012, the Southern Poverty and Law Center identified over 1000 active hate groups in the United States, with at least two in each state), as is covert racism, especially in the form of institutionalized discrimination. What many in the black community may be forgetting is the distinction between de jure discrimination, which has its origins in law like the old Jim Crow traditions versus de facto discrimination, which is discrimination by effect. Any policy, practice, process, or protocol that systematically has a disproportionately negative impact on one group defined by race or ethnicity is discriminatory in a defacto manner regardless of intent: noble or malicious.

These four factors of (1) narcissism, (2) feelings within the black community that all is okay or that we have now arrived, (3) no sense about controlled spending and growing wealth, and (4) the lack of perceived need for viable and sustained black leadership—all point to a psychological condition among the masses of black people in America. This condition is analogous to a type of unhealed trauma, but only it inflicts an entire community of people, i.e., it is a macro-level affliction. This four-pronged affliction interacts with our history and further complicates the matter.

Think about it. In this country, blacks have been victims of 246 years of chattel slavery (1619–1865), followed by 71 years of Jim Crow racism and discrimination (1883–1954), 40 years of advancement (1865–1882 and 1954–1977), and 34 years of denial, feeling like all is well (1980–2014). That is 317 years of severe psychological trauma, 40 years of positive feelings, and 34 years post the stress with no healing and being in denial. There is no wonder that we want immediate gratification. After hundreds of years of systematic and sustained denial of the American dream, blacks want to look and feel successful immediately, right now, today! This is not an excuse; let's understand it. We don't want to delay gratification by saving or investing money and growing a business. Why do that, when many blacks make a good wage and can buy a Lexus, nice clothes, house, and entertainment toys and be successful now? Yet, we are typically missing the aspect of wealth generation.

The black community needs macro-level psychological healing. I believe that the psychological healing will naturally occur when the black community begins, through empowerment and self-determination, to take steps to improve its own condition. The Black Triangle, discussed later in this chapter, is one such intervention that could help to bring about that healing process in my estimation.

Speaking of psychological healing for the black community, what are the mechanisms of action or underlying dynamics at work that make operating from a point of view of immediate gratification so compelling? According to a January 2013 issue of *Scientific America,* new research in the discipline of neuroeconomics is currently investigating some of these dynamics and mechanisms. Researchers at Washington University in St. Louis are blazing the trail in this new avenue of research. With the use of functional magnetic resonance imaging techniques, brain activity is being explored in individuals who are prone to immediate gratification versus those more inclined to delay gratification. Early work has shown more neural activity in the anterior prefrontal cortex of the brain for those who can easily delay gratification.

One theory about why things in the immediate future are more appealing to some has to do with the fact that the details are clearer when the outcome is proximal. As the outcome becomes more distal, then the details about it become fuzzy, decreasing the attractiveness in people who do not like to delay gratification. Let me be clear that I am not in any way suggesting that this research will necessarily lead to a strategy that can be applied to the black community. This is just an interesting aside that demonstrates that one day, we might know more about the mechanics involved in immediate versus delayed gratification.

# THREATS TO THE SUCCESS OF BARACK OBAMA'S PRESIDENCY – ILLUSTRATION OF THE CURRENT WHITE BACKLASH PHENOMENON?

Presidents of the United States are elected by a majority of the popular vote usually and always by a majority of the Electoral College vote. This means that by definition, whenever a president is elected to office, there is a faction of the American populace that did not support the president by voting for him. Despite this fact, most past presidents have typically reached a point early on in their tenures when most of the public tends to rally around them and hope for the best out of respect for the office and realizing that a sitting president once elected is everyone's president. This has not necessarily been the case for Barack Obama.

When President Barack Obama took office in his first term in January of 2009, the narrative of American history was never to be the same. Arguably there were many things about the Obama presidency that were different, but one of the most striking is the unprecedented effort spent to derail his success. All presidents have their naysayers, but time spent to thwart Mr. Obama has been unparalleled.

In fact, things started before he took office in 2009. The Tea Party movement actually started during the administration of George W. Bush when he rescued banks as per the October 2008 Troubled Asset Relief Program bank bailout. The Tea Party's origin was a blend of conservative, libertarian, and populist ideologies. But make no mistake about it, the Tea Party movement's fervor and momentum were synergized by the arrival of Mr. Obama in the Oval Office, when it started registering major objections to federal government spending in the 2009 Stimulus Bill and the Health Care Reform Bill of 2010. Who in the black community thought a black or half-black president that looks 100 percent black would have smooth sailing,even in the twenty-first century?

The assaults on President Obama personally and on his policies have been relentless. There have been questions about his nationality to daily assaults on his policies by Fox News commentators. Shannon Richardson of Texas mailed ricin to the president in May of 2013. Marine sergeant Gary Stein started the Armed Forces Tea Party and, in 2012, said he would not follow Obama's orders as commander and chief and invoked the First Amendment as his protection. Rock and roll artist Ted Nugent said if Obama were reelected he (supposedly himself) would soon thereafter be dead or in jail. Further, Nugent said after the Obama reelection that America had voted for spiritual and economic suicide. Then there was Republican primary candidate Herman Cain who was pitted as an answer to Obama. Condoleezza Rice addressed the National Republican Convention in an effort to upstage Barack and Michelle, and then conservatives propped up Dr. Ben Carson against Obama and the Affordable Care Act. Dr. Carson made the comparison between the Affordable Care Act and slavery, equating the two as similarly detrimental. United States citizens in at least thirty states across the nation signed succession petitions after Mr. Obama was reelected. The Southern Poverty Law Center maintains that anti-government "patriot" groups increased in number 800 percent during Mr. Obama's first presidency.

There have also been some larger scale efforts to bring down Mr. Obama and his presidency. It seems that Republican members of the United States Congress have vowed to obstruct any and all initiatives that come out of the White House from the Obama administration. Billionaire businessmen, the Koch brothers, had committed to do whatever they could to ensure Obama was not elected for a second term, and now that he has been reelected, they are throwing their financial muscle behind everything that is either anti-Obama or anti-black. For example, allegedly they paid for George Zimmerman's legal defense.

Republicans, promoting the agenda of Tea Party conservatives, shut down the government at the end of the last federal fiscal year on September 30, 2013, in an unsuccessful effort to force Obama Care to be repealed. President Obama said the Republicans were determined to deny health insurance coverage to the projected 30 million individuals who would be newly insured as a result of Obama Care. Further, the president termed efforts to repeal Obama Care a Republican Party rallying initiative. Beyond this, Republicans threatened to not raise the country's debt ceiling, a routine maneuver that allows the nation to pay its bills.

One of the more formidable threats to Obama and his presidency has come from the National Rifle Association (NRA) in response to his efforts to put forth reasonable measures for gun control in the wake of a rash of gun violence and deaths, especially the Newtown, Connecticut, tragedy. I assert that much of this renewed passion over protecting the Second Amendment and resisting gun control is in direct response to Obama's reelection and his audacity to tamper with what many call an inalienable right. I believe the clear implication by the NRA and its members in their over the top rhetoric is that we need our guns because we may have to overthrow the United States government with Obama at the helm. This is a case of the Second Amendment right being taken too far.

Here are five realities that speak to the fallacy of the Second Amendment. (1) If you have an overwhelming desire to own a gun for a reason other than sports or recreation, then you have a proclivity toward violence (view violent solutions as okay) because you have already come to grips with the fact that there are situations when the use of deadly force by you is acceptable. I am willing to bet that all such instances would not be legal and appropriate uses of a gun. Truly law-abiding and peaceful people have no need for guns and believe guns are for law enforcement and the military. (2) You have no business with a gun if you believe that overthrowing the United States government may be necessary. Two hundred and thirty or so years ago, this thinking may have been reasonable when things were formative and less stable in this country, but now, no way. If this applies to you, then you are a threat to our way of life. (3) Anyone can claim to be a law-abiding citizen under normal circumstances, but in a moment's notice under certain duress, we can all be pushed to a point of impaired judgment and become a menace to society. So personally, I do not buy the "I'm a law-abiding citizen" line. Furthermore, individuals who are truly mentally ill, as in having a long-term mental illness such as schizophrenia, are statistically less likely to be violent with or without a gun than the general population. Therefore, this push to limit guns for the mentally ill is a misguided oversimplification of the issue. (4) There is nothing sacred or beyond reproach that was framed in the Constitution by its conceivers. After all, they were fallible men dealing with a much simpler and homogeneous society then and claiming to be all-knowing and virtuous. Remember, they were slave masters while preaching inalienable rights. So I am in no way enamored by their wisdom. Consider that anything written is time bound, which means the context of the time when it was written drives its meaning and interpretation. Back then, there was a need for every citizen to be armed. Now, it is not the case. (5) The right to bear arms is not a God-given right. God has absolutely nothing to do with America's gun obsession. That responsibility lies on the shoulders of aggressive men with too much bravado. Guns are the problem because people are fallible, always have been and always will be. Just think about the number of suicides (over 19,000 per year according to 2011 data from the CDC's National Center for Health Statistics and over 60 percent of all gun deaths) and unintended/accidental deaths each year (over 800 deaths) in the United States. If guns were not so available, these lives could be saved.

Now, is there a connection between the NRA and all those red-blooded American gun enthusiasts and the fact that President Obama receives thirty death threats a day? Are those that threaten the president planning to beat, stab, or stone him to death? I think not. Guns would be their weapon of choice. Surely, all United States presidents receive death threats. However, according to Ronald Kessler's 2009 book, *The President's Secret Service*, the level of threats received by Mr. Obama represents a 400 percent increase over the number of threats his predecessor, President George W. Bush, routinely received.

## EXAMPLES OF THE MAGNITUDE OF THE CHALLENGE OF IMPROVING THE BLACK CONDITION

I have two examples to share that I believe illustrate the magnitude of the challenge of change that the black community must bring about to survive in the twenty-first century. Both examples address how to prepare, equip, and shape young people in the black community who are the next generation of black leaders to be in a position to facilitate the kind of positive change needed to bring about economic, health, and social parity with majority populations in this country. To me, this is about succession planning, i.e., preparing those who will lead the way for the black community to reach a better place in the future. I think these two examples are particularly compelling illustrations of the work that must be done to turn things around. The first illustration I call, "Who Is Crazy, Him or Me?: the Wendy's Gang Banger Example." The second one I have titled, "Kids Are Impressionable: the Taco Bell/Bill Gates Example."

## WENDY'S EXAMPLE

One day, maybe seventeen years ago, I was in a Wendy's fast-food restaurant around lunchtime. Immediately in front of me in line was a young black male who looked to be in his late teens or early twenties. Based on my biases and assumptions about him from what I could glean from his dress and assumptive forms (amount of bling he wore, his posture and walk, the car he drove with bling rims, etc.), I decided that he was probably a drug dealer (shame on me!). Next, my perceptions were confirmed in my own mind when he pulled out a wad of cash to pay for his meal that looked to have easily been one thousand dollars or more. Then, I started thinking about the fact that I, a PhD then director of a statewide public health program, had about $10 in my pocket at the most and my debit card.

This young man obtained his food and went on as did I. Then, I began to think about what the conversation would be like if, hypothetically, I could have gotten him to agree to sit and talk to me for a while. I imagined that in the conversation, it would be revealed that he is not employed in a traditional job, but makes fast money. I would then share my profession.

Moving on, I imagined the conversation would progress to the topic of me asking him why he had decided to pursue making fast money as his livelihood? I am not sure what he would have said, but I would have encouraged him to think about pursuing a more traditional, legal, safe career preparation path (trade school or college) and then find a traditional job he enjoyed. I then thought, he would probably look at me, size me up based on how I was dressed, what I was driving (a nondescript Saturn), and how much cash I had in my pocket, and laughed.

He might have then countered and asked me how many years I had gone to school and then inquired when was the last time I held several thousand dollars of cash in my hands?

In the end, I concluded that other than the important point that my career was legal and I was not as likely to face an untimely violent demise, he was about as likely to convince me to join his profession as I was in convincing him to do something different. Additionally, in consideration of the fact that most young people perceive themselves as invincible and immortal (i.e., nothing bad will happen to me), he was probably as firm in his conviction and career direction as I was in my own.

Subsequently, I realized that I was woefully ill equipped and inept in that I, with years of formal education and well steeped in making cogent arguments, would probably not have been able to say anything to convince that young man to change his life direction. It immediately became apparent that my inability was exactly the reason why we as a black community cannot effectively persuade many young people to amend their ways and pursue what we believe would be a more appropriate course in life. At that point, I truly recognized that changing a generation of young people was a formidable task at best. I concluded that I could not have persuaded this young man and, therefore, had little reason to believe that others with my mission would be more successful.

## TACO BELL EXAMPLE

One evening about eleven years ago, my son who was five at the time and one of his friends and I were dining in a Taco Bell fast-food restaurant. (I guess by now, you can see that I like fast food.) My son, his friend, and I were in line, again, behind a young black male who pulled out an unbelievable amount of cash. This guy looked to have easily, in my quick estimation, three to four thousand dollars or more in his pocket. He had a toddler with him that called him daddy. This twenty-something young man seemed to be a bit immature. At one point, he loudly announced that he had enough money to buy everything on the menu for everyone in the restaurant, including the workers several times over.

At the point that this gentleman pulled out his roll of cash, I noticed my son's and his friend's eyes get big. They wanted to comment right then and there, but I immediately shut them down. Once we had our food and were at our table a comfortable distance from everyone else, we resumed that conversation. My son said, "Dad, that guy must be rich, did you see all the money he had?" I nodded and stated, "Yes, I saw it, son, but…" Then, I proceeded to give both my son and his friend a lesson.

The lesson was that people who are truly rich or wealthy do not carry around and flash large rolls of cash. I explained to both youth that Bill Gates or Warren Buffet, real men of wealth, would never carry that large of a sum of cash. I further explained that truly wealthy people don't show it off in that way. They have moderate amounts of cash and credit or debit cards on their person and keep their assets in banks, stocks, or other investments and income-earning vehicles. My son and his friend seemed to follow some of what I was saying, keeping in mind that they were all of five years old at the time. However, I could see that they were still mesmerized and impressed by seeing that large of a sum of cash.

This immediately made me think about the power of visual trappings of success. This I remembered was why in the hood drug dealers are looked up to by so many young black males who are at that impressionable age. Think about it, if you live in an inner city housing project and you are a black male up to the teen years, you have limited repeat exposure to positive black male role models. The only black male role models that are easily accessible are successful black men on the television, and before President Obama, these were primarily athletes or entertainers. The black males in the community that one could talk to and interact with were those who looked successful, i.e., drug dealers and those pursuing fast money.

Drug dealers have that undeniable visible look of success, especially to the young and impressionable. That look is based on their swagger (i.e., how they talk, lean and carry themselves), how they dress (bling and pants hanging down), and their assumptive forms (gun in the waistband, plenty of time to stand around and do nothing, the conspicuous cars they drive, the cash they flash, and the girl on the arm when it is time to party). And we wonder why young black males who live in inner cities have limited aspirations to careers other than being athletes, rappers and other entertainers, or drug dealers. It is human nature. People are influenced by those to whom they have immediate and routine access. The psychologists among us will recognize this type of influence as part of the social learning theory, which accounts for how most of us learn and are socialized by those in our immediate environments as we grow and develop from infants. This part of human nature is truly a challenge and what a major challenge it is.

The above two experiences made me realize that we have a lot of work to do in guiding black youth. On the one hand, we have to find effective strategies to reach those youth who are not under our parental purview. On the other hand, those youth to whom we parent are not guaranteed success either, as they are equally captive to the negative motivators that are pervasive in our community. This challenge is formidable. We also need more effective tools to be able to wage persuasive arguments.

# TEN COMMON-SENSE STRATEGIES FOR BLACK COMMUNITY SELF-IMPROVEMENT: BLACK TRIANGLE

There are no panaceas or easy answers when it comes to what will work to cure the ills of the black community. As the title of Nelson Mandela's book, *No Easy Walk to Freedom* (1985), suggests, there is no shortcut. I have assembled what, in my humble opinion, represents a collection of common-sense strategies. They are necessarily simplistic because they would have to be in order for me to propose them. More importantly, they must resonate with all blacks regardless of social, economic, and educational exposure.

Specifically, my thinking in this regard parallels Abraham Maslow's famous hierarchy of needs (1970), in which he stressed the importance of addressing basic and primary needs before moving to address higher order more evolved needs. What I have proposed is a hierarchy of sorts, but I call it a triangle, the Black Triangle (see figure 1). However, the logic and symbolism are similar to Maslow's work in that there are several levels that could either be addressed sequentially, or deviating from Maslow's thinking, all ten strategies could be addressed concurrently. Whether to proceed sequentially up the levels or to tackle all ten simultaneously really depends on the speed at which results are desired and the level of commitment garnered. For example, if commitment is tentative, then proceeding stepwise up the levels might be best to achieve some early incremental success. Alternatively, if there is enough broad-based enthusiasm and commitment, all ten steps could be tackled at once in which case total black community improvement could be achieved faster.

There are four levels of strategies. Level 1 strategies are those primarily focused on new learning for blacks. Level 2 strategies are fewer and focused on providing support to black entities. That is, both support in terms of helping to develop new entities as in supporting entrepreneurs who start new black businesses as well as sustaining existing entities as in black colleges and universities. Level 3 strategies are fewer and focus on making key personal decisions to advance the community. At level 4, there is only one strategy that may be the most difficult to build a broad base of buy-in for because it centers on donating personal resources for the good of the cause.

All four levels of strategies require discipline and commitment across the black community to achieve an adequate dose of widespread implementation within each level to be efficacious. This would be the case whether using the gradual and sequential or the rapid implementation approach to black community self enhancement. I will discuss levels starting at the bottom of the triangle first as the foundation to the approach and then proceed upward vertically.

## LEVEL 1 OF THE TRIANGLE

At the base or bottom of the triangle are four strategies. The first strategy is to maximize education levels throughout the black community. This is a learning-focused strategy. It does not mean that everyone must attend graduate or professional school nor obtain an undergraduate degree for that matter. It does mean that each member of the black community needs to display first and foremost a commitment to acquiring the optimal level of formal training needed to reach the top of their chosen profession. For many, this may mean a technical, trade school, or an apprenticeship. We, as a people, must be committed to excellence in the manner of everyone having the best credentials possible to be exceptionally qualified for professional pursuits. The obvious barrier to implementation of this strategy, assuming buy-in, is funding. However, most formal training and education programs currently have sources of financial aid to assist needy, motivated, and goal-directed students. We must avail ourselves of these sources of support as needed.

The second strategy on level 1 of the triangle (the bottom) is also a learning-based strategy. It involves making a commitment to have everyone in the black community to become more familiar with our history. This is long overdue. We already have Black History Month in February, so this is not a new idea. However, we must devote ourselves to learning about and making sure our youth learn about the vast and great contributions of people of African descent around the globe year round. Once we are aware of our legacy of greatness, it will be difficult to hold back that innate greatness that resides in each one of us. A good book that should be required reading for all blacks is Chancellor Williams' 1987 work, *The Destruction of Black Civilization*.

Strategy three on level 1 entails every black person learning about money. As a people we must learn to discern the difference between making a purchase that can accumulate value over time (property, land, equities, precious metals) and those that depreciate (cars, most jewelry, clothes, weaves, nails, tattoos, rims, alligator shoes, technology gadgets, toys, etc.). Not only must we know the difference, but then we must exercise some discipline in refraining from purchases that equate to flushing money down the toilet. This might require some of that healing because we have already discussed the compulsion in the black community toward immediate gratification. We must also learn about credit, debt (avoid payday loans like the plaque), saving, investing, and living within a budget. Ultimately, we must come to understand that the person who has the most is not always the person who earns the most.

A lot of what people have in terms of assets and wealth has to do with knowing how to keep a high percentage of what you earn and then having that money begin to earn more. I was once a member of an all-black male investment club, the Expectation Investment Club in Richmond, Virginia, and at least one of our members (maybe more) was a millionaire. He was not a highly educated man, not formerly so, and though he made a good income, he was not the highest paid person. Nevertheless, he understood money and knew how to make it grow and have it leverage other resources. He did not deny himself creature comforts, but he exercised fiscal discipline and timing. I would put that individual in charge of teaching the black community about money.

Beyond this, I think a subscription to Black Enterprise and a copy of the 2006 book, *The Millionaire Next Door* by Thomas Stanley and William Danko would be necessary items in every black home or to be read in public libraries. In their book, Stanley and Danko talk about the dual strategy of earning more and spending less as well as the fact that 8 out of 10 millionaires are first generation rich, 1 in 5 is retired, and half of them own a business. Black investment clubs are also a great vehicle for learning about money as it relates to investing. They offer a supportive and nurturing environment for sharing among advanced and novice members.

Okay, I have to resist the urge to get on my soapbox with the fourth strategy on level 1. Black people must learn that every situation that involves different races is not racist and does not pertain to racism. Let me say this one more time, because I know someone is unable to hear this. Every situation that involves a black and a white man, for example, does not necessarily involve intentions motivated by racism. The first step in understanding this is for blacks to recognize that white people are not the only ones who can be racist. All people can be racist, remember the title of this book? Racism is a human phenomenon, and no one group owns a majority share of the market. It just so happens that because of historical events in this country over the last almost 400 years, we have grown accustomed to racism that is perpetrated by whites toward blacks. This, however, does not mean that blacks or any other group cannot be racist. You can look at every country in Africa and see that racism or a dynamic very similar based on power or class is a pervasive social phenomenon. And of course, racism clearly exists in America, but when you conclude that the problems in 99 out of 100 situations are based on racism, you lose your credibility and people stop listening.

Here is a recent case in point. Not long ago, the national news indicated that our beloved Oprah Winfrey had concluded that she had been a victim of racism. A merchant in Switzerland denied her the ability to see a handbag with a $30,000+ price tag. The salesperson involved apparently had made the determination looking at Oprah that she could not afford such an item. The woman obviously did not recognize Oprah. Now, was this a clear instance of racism or were there other plausible explanations for why Oprah was not allowed to see this merchandise? No one will ever know for certain, but Oprah reportedly was convinced that racism is the one and only explanation for the sequence of events. However, to unequivocally call it racism may be a mistake. This is a perfect example of what I am referring to. So Oprah's cultural bias, as it relates to racism, kicked in, and if the salesperson actually acted based on racism, then her cultural bias kicked in as well. This is why I say we are all racists. The bottom line is that no one, including probably the salesperson, knows for sure what dynamics were at work in that situation. So, it is a mistake to assume it has to have been the race explanation.

The key to overcoming this automatic conclusion that many blacks seem pre-programmed to reach is to take our reactions out of the autopilot mode. We must begin to reserve judgment and consciously analyze and think before arriving at a conclusion. A black man is shot by a white man, and we automatically assume it was a racially motivated assault. A black employee is terminated from a job by a white manager; we are convinced it was due to racism. I was stranded on the highway while driving a white car, it must have been racism. You see what a slippery slope this can become? We must evaluate each situation based on its unique facts and evidence and resist the urge to rush to judgment that something was racially motivated and arrive at that conclusion later, if and when all other hypotheses have been exhausted and the evidence clearly suggests racism. It should not be the first thing that comes to mind or out of our mouths. This happens, I believe, because of the healing that needs to occur in our community. Clearly, there are other reasons beyond racism that account for unfortunate outcomes in situations where parties of different races are involved.

## LEVEL 2 OF THE TRIANGLE

There are three strategies on level 2 of the triangle, keeping in mind that we are moving from the bottom up. The first strategy on level 2 is to emphasize among our youth the idea of entrepreneurship. No longer is it enough to go to school and prepare to obtain the best job you can acquire working for someone else. That was the goal in my generation. Our kids need to think about building their own businesses as an ultimate goal. We still need to work for others to gain needed experience, but the final destination should be to work for ourselves. The key to successful implementation of this strategy is first and foremost to begin to shift the way we think about work and in turn begin to talk to our youth about work differently. Certainly, start-up capital is always a challenge, but it is pretty much for everyone inside or outside of the black community. I know some have it easier. We need to begin tapping into current resources designated to help like the Small Business Administration of the federal government.

Providing support to black institutions is the next level 2 strategy. By institutions, I mean primarily educational entities such as black preparatory or charter schools and, of course, historically black colleges and universities. It is particularly important to support these educational institutions at the undergraduate level. Many do not have expansive graduate or professional school programs, and teaching at the undergraduate level tends to be their primary mission as opposed to research. Black educational institutions typically provide the nurturing and sense of black identity and community that black youth need before embarking on the big, pluralistic, white-dominated society called America. There are also other black-owned and -operated institutions that we should support such as media entities or any other type of business that is large, established, and has institutional status.

Beyond supporting black institutions, we need to be sure to purchase black and patronize black businesses as the third level 2 strategy. This includes merchants and professionals like physicians, dentists, attorneys, accountants, mechanics, etc. I know that sometimes it is difficult to overcome the perception that the white business is inherently better. Again, this is part of the healing that needs to occur. A lot of times, such feelings are manifestations of internalized racism. We have been denigrated so systemically and for so long that in many cases we have begun to believe the hype, that we are inferior to whites. This is a natural response after a while. Then, there are some whites who believe this and then maintain these positions under the guise of science like the authors Richard Herrnstein and Charles Murray of the 1994 book, *The Bell Curve*. That book made some explicit and implicit assertions about the role of intelligence in the lack of broad-based achievement among blacks in this country and linked low intelligence to social ills among other claims.

Sometimes, supporting black-owned businesses requires some sacrifice. Often, the merchandise is more expensive because black businesses do not always have in-roads to the best wholesalers or suppliers. Our businesses certainly heretofore have not been able to buy in large enough quantity to obtain volume-based discounts. And then, because we are relative newbies to running businesses compared to our white counterparts, sometimes we lack sophistication in marketing and offering creative financing packages. These things come with time and will improve for black businesses in the future.

I can clearly remember some years ago patronizing a black furniture store, knowing I was paying more for some merchandise, but in my mind, I rationalized that if I and people who look like me did not support that business no one else would. Clearly, white customers were not at that time patronizing that business. So I paid a price to support my own, but it was worth it in my estimation. This is the type of sacrifice that I believe we must increasingly be willing to make in the near term until black businesses catch up to majority businesses.

## LEVEL 3 OF THE TRIANGLE

On level 3 of the triangle, the stakes are higher because it calls for two strategies that require true dedication to black community improvement. The first strategy will be viewed by some as controversial. It involves blacks making a conscious decision to marry black. This has nothing to do with arguments in support of racial purity nor is it anti-white or anti–mixed race couples. It has to do with economics and making a concerted effort to begin to keep dollars generated by black families in the black community. Anyone who has eyes open in 2014 in urban areas can see that interracial dating and marriage are becoming more and more acceptable. Though this strategy may have implications for dating practices, it really focuses on the decision of a marriage partner. For example, I dated interracially in college and after, but have been married only to two black women.

I recognize that this strategy will be a hard sell for many Generation X'ers (the twenty-somethings) because they have not lived in a time when there were no interracial marriages. Today, one only has to look at any professional sport and can routinely see black athletes who have taken on nonblack brides. Again, I am not condemning this in principle, but believe that the more we can do to keep the dollars earned by blacks directly benefiting black people, the more we can "pull ourselves up by our bootstraps," to borrow from Booker T. Washington's approach for "Negro" self-improvement. Consider the fact that Jews, Asians, and Arabs who are living in this country by and large marry primarily within their groups. I recognize that there is a certain forbidden lure involved in black-white interracial relationships since miscegenation was illegal for so long.

The second strategy on level 3 is to engage in black gentrification. This is another strategy that will be difficult for many blacks to buy into. However, blacks need to consider moving back to the cities or alternatively stop the mass exodus from cities to suburban America. We need to take back the cities and have a positive presence. Most of the challenges in the black community (poverty, crime, homelessness, etc.) are concentrated in cities. Moving back or not leaving urban areas in the first place puts us in proximity to be able to exert more black community positive influence. There is one other reason why it is absolutely critical that blacks take back the cities, and it has to do with mentoring.

I made an interesting observation when I was a member of that all-black male investment club that I mentioned previously. We held monthly club meetings, and they rotated and were hosted at the homes of our members. My first year as a club member, I immediately noticed that with few exceptions—very few—the members of the club each lived in the most expensive all or mostly white suburban neighborhoods that they could afford. Now, these were positive, hardworking, law-abiding, and successful black men. Success in their minds or the notion of "having arrived" apparently meant living in middle and upper class almost all-white neighborhoods.

The problem with this practice is that they had effectively removed themselves from being proximal role models to young black boys in the inner city, leaving them with only role models on the television (athletes and entertainers) and men in their communities with the tangible look of success, i.e., adult males making fast and mostly illegal money. If we could have black men and their families to continue to reside in their communities of origin regardless of how affluent they become, then inner city boys who need to be inspired and mentored will have ready access to positive adult black men. Soon, young black boys in the cities will begin to want to be teachers, computer programmers, corporate factory workers, electricians, professors, etc., and a world of possibilities in terms of careers will open. Back then, when I made this observation in the investment club, I did not mention it to club members because I wanted to continue observing and noticing things as they naturally occurred.

## LEVEL 4 OF THE TRIANGLE

At the final top level of the triangle, there is only one strategy. I call this strategy the "1-300 Plan." In involves the top 1 percent of the most affluent blacks in the nation (approximately 390,000 individuals)[1] donating 1 percent of their gross annual income (approximately $8000)[2] once, and this equates to $3.12 billion dollars total. (It would actually be more dollars because 1 percent of annual income for many blacks would be more than $8,000.) This money would then be divided up and allocated to the top 300 cities in the United States, which are those cities with populations of at least 100,000.[3] Such cities would also, and most importantly, have black communities of substantial size. This gives each of those cities $10.4 million[4] to put aside in a black education/training and entrepreneurship fund. Then, the black community governance structure in each of the 300 cities would be allowed to allocate no more than $1 million dollars annually to support black education/training and business startup. The remaining funds in the startup year ($9.4 million) would be invested and grow (in a low-risk high-yield investment vehicle), and the money would last as long as it lasts, but hopefully ten to twenty years.

Ten to twenty years of this kind of capital investment strategically placed in these cities to support black education/training and business startup would represent a bolus dose of resources that would have to positively impact and advance the black community across the nation. There would have to be some type of centralized nonprofit organizing/oversight structure (with 501c3 status) set up nationally to implement this strategy along with a companion entity in each of the 300 designated cities to ensure that funds are received and properly deployed to support primarily the strategies of (1) educating/training of blacks and (2) black business entrepreneurship/start-up. Other uses of the money consistent with these two strategies might be deemed appropriate by the governing councils in the designated cities.

The "1-300 Plan" is just a concept at this point and there are lots of operational details that would have to be firmed up before something of this magnitude could be launched. It is an ambitious plan to say the least. It does place initial responsibility on the top 1 percent of affluent blacks, but keep in mind this is a one-time donation to a nonprofit entity (i.e., a tax-deductible donation). This is not unlike W. E. B. Dubois' concept of the "Talented Tenth," except here you could call it the "Affluent One Percent." This strategy would require a sense of community, commitment, and sharing that probably does not exist currently, but if a few well-known blacks start the process, hopefully, others in the top 1 percent would follow and volunteer to participate.

This plan involves blacks helping themselves, and this could have a nice cathartic feel for us all that could contribute to our healing. I believe this plan is a lot more probable and feasible than expecting white America to pay reparations, which is what Randall Robinson called for in his eloquently written 2001 book, *The Debt: What America Owes to Blacks*. While it is true that America does owe reparations to blacks, waiting for actual payment would appear to be a no-win proposition.

If the ten strategies of the Black Triangle plan are actually launched at some point, it would behoove us to evaluate the resulting success. Such an endeavor might be as simple as revisiting those eleven data indices ("indices of oppression in the black community") presented in the table earlier in this chapter at say ten, fifteen, and twenty years down the road to see what has changed.

Figure 1 - "Black Triangle": Ten Community Self Help Strategies in the 21st Century

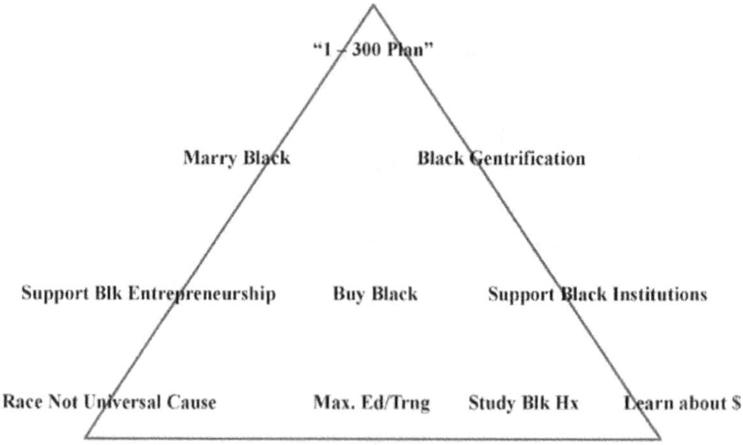

# LOOKING FORWARD

## HEALTH IMPERATIVE IN THE BLACK COMMUNITY

Before looking forward, admittedly, the one area that I have not discussed to this point is the health imperative in the black community. In chapter 4 in the section on the "Current Status of the Black Condition: A Data Perspective," an implication that could have easily been drawn was the fact that the health status of the black community is not on par with that of the white community. This is, in fact, the case. Much of this challenge has to do with the black community's intergenerational response to oppression, poverty, and life stressors. I hypothesized this to be the case in my published Disability Disparities model (2009 – see figure 2)[5] where I maintain this intergenerational phenomenon (in Domain 1) is part of the reason why blacks have higher incidence of chronic medical conditions and disabilities.

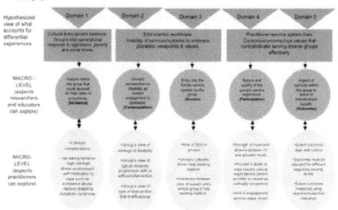

**Disability Disparities Model**

The primary origin of this intergenerational response to oppression, poverty, and life stress is lifestyle considerations. For example, the conditions of heart disease and stroke that blacks have high incidence of emanate directly from metabolic syndrome, which is increased risk due directly to obesity, hypertension, and high levels of cholesterol. Each of these precursor risk factors derive from a sedentary lifestyle and unhealthy eating. In addition, living in high stress and high poverty communities can promote excessive eating, drinking, and drug use as coping strategies or a way to self-medicate. It is also well-known that there is a high concentration of liquor and fast-food restaurants in black communities. There is also a paucity of healthy eating alternatives such as Panera Bread, Trader Joe's, or Whole Foods establishments. In fact, some call black communities "food deserts" because of the dearth of healthy eating options.

The solution that I am proposing is a holistic approach to improved health in the black community. As an organizing framework, I am suggesting the holistic model developed

# We are All Racists:
## the Truth about Cultural Bias

by Sharon Wegscheider-Cruse as presented in her 1981 book, *Another Chance: Hope and Help for the Alcoholic Family*. Wegscheider-Cruse proposes six dimensions where attention is needed to become a healthy and balanced person: (1) physical, (2) mental, (3) emotional, (4) social, (5) spiritual, and (6) volitional. As a starting point in addressing the health imperative in the black community, I am suggesting a specific strategy for each of the six dimensions in Wegscheider-Cruse's model. Keep in mind that I am taking the liberty of suggesting use of Wegscheider-Cruse's model on a macro-, community level, though she developed it for individual or micro-level use.

For the physical dimension, blacks need to give more attention to fully understanding the health and disability disparities phenomena. Next, we need to commit ourselves to healthy living that includes regular exercise, proper nutrition, and adequate rest. This includes annual visits to a health care provider for a routine physical examination as well as availing ourselves of all early and routine screenings for known health conditions.

For the mental dimension, we need to devote ourselves to more effective stress management, which of course, routine exercise helps with immensely. We can supplement the exercise with yoga and meditation as well as learn our best individualized coping strategies including positive self-talk. We need to supplant current unhealthy stress management outlets such as compulsive overeating, drinking, gambling, and using drugs with more healthy alternatives (i.e., positive hobbies).

Our emotional healing will be tied to the extent to which we learn to appropriately express all of our feelings and stop repressing our emotional expressions. If we can engage in some community-wide healing of our collective damaged black psyche, then this will help as well. Understanding our history and participating in the Black Triangle strategies discussed in the previous chapter will be of benefit. These two strategies will also enhance us socially. For the social dimension, we need to additionally embrace a greater sense of collective consciousness as a people. I submit that this will naturally happen to some degree as we learn more about our past history of collectivism as a people.

In terms of spirituality, blacks already have a deep tradition and strong devotion to our spiritual lives, which we must continue. I believe we would benefit from a stronger relationship with God and de-emphasize some of the current relationships we have with man (pastors) and man-made religious organizations (churches). This will not be a popular recommendation, but the big picture is that our salvation depends on the quality of our direct relationship with God and our works, and not the quality of relationships with self-appointed envoys of God.

To improve our volition, we must be clear on our power as a people. That is power particularly when it comes to economics (i.e., our purchasing power) and voting. We need to be more empowered and self-determining in setting our own social, political, educational, and economic agendas and seeking our own collective destiny as a people. The more we can think and learn to function collectively as a community, the more we will be empowered and self-determining as a people.

## GEORGE ZIMMERMAN AND MICHAEL DUNN LEGAL CASES

There is one more issue salient to the health of the black community that I am compelled to address. That issue is the endangerment of young black males. This is not a new topic. Dr. Jawanza Kunjufu has written consistently about what he calls "the conspiracy to destroy black boys" and his work began with his four volume series first published in 1982 titled Countering the Conspiracy to Destroy Black Boys. Though my natural inclination is not to jump wholeheartedly on the conspiracy theory bandwagon, United States history is replete with examples that could provide evidence to validate such a theory (e.g., Rodney King, Amadou Diallo and others). One merely needs to examine rates of assaults, murders, arrests and convictions of young black males in the United States since it became a nation in 1776 to see patterns that might substantiate such a theory.

Most notably now; however, is the beginning pattern of black male teenagers killed in situations by non-black citizens who really had no business interacting with these youths, and the legal system's reluctance to hold these perpetrators accountable. Some might argue that this pattern is also not new (e.g., Emmett Till), offering as evidence longstanding perceptions of black males as threats held by some in the majority culture. In this new century, the cases of George Zimmerman in the killing of Trayvon Martin and the case of Michael Dunn in the killing of Jordan Davis have continued that pattern and captured the nation's attention. In the black community, these two cases were vivid reminders that black males can be killed with little or no accountability. The two cases occurred less than a year apart, and in these situations white men were found not guilty of killing these young black teenagers. In both cases, culture and arguably cultural bias in the form of racism played an undeniable, multi-dimensional role.

In the Zimmerman and Dunn cases, there were stark differences in the worldviews between the perpetrators and the victims in terms of race, age, view of appropriate dress in the Zimmerman case, view of appropriate music in the Dunn case, and in verbal interaction patterns (i.e., the parties were unable to reach an appropriate conflict resolution short of violence). With both incidents, the legal system attempted, as it typically does, to function in a culture-neutral vacuum of dealing with the facts only, but realistically this can never happen. Operating in a true culture-free manner is never possible in the human realm.

On several levels, these two cases exhibited cultural clashes based primarily on the type of bias called racism. In both situations, the perpetrators held racially motivated animus toward their victims. Zimmerman viewed black males dressed in hoodies traveling at night as suspicious. Dunn viewed rap music as listened to by black males as inherently thuggish. So, in many ways, the stage for confrontation was predetermined by the two perpetrator's preconceived notions (i.e., racial biases) about black males.

Race was also a point of difference in terms of the general public's expectations about the legal proceedings and desires about the outcomes going into these trials. Some viewed the Zimmerman case as being similar to the O.J. Simpson case in terms of the inextricable racial dynamics. There were those who viewed the Dunn case as another Zimmerman-like scenario. Still others felt the travesty in the Zimmerman trial could not possibly repeat itself in the Dunn trial.

During the Dunn trial, race played a role in the ruling made by the presiding judge that previously written letters by Dunn that were laced with racially derogatory language could not be admissible evidence. Also, race clearly impacted the way both the defense and prosecution teams prepared for and tried these cases. Post-trial reactions, media commentary, public opinion as well as whether these cases would be appealed were arguably all influenced by race factors.

These two recent cases offer more evidence that cultural bias related to race is still alive and well in the United States. There is heightened concern, at least in the black community, about the seemingly increasing victimization of young black males as a result of racial bias and the fact that the legal system appears to be unwilling to adequately address these atrocities. We have heard so much about the "stand your ground" self-defense standard. What about adopting a new standard of "everyone minding their own business"? Now, more than ever, we all need to understand our own vulnerability to cultural bias, find ways to bridge our differences by accentuating our commonalities, and when all else fails, put down the guns and mind our own affairs.

## INTERESTING DEVELOPMENTS

The notion of cultural bias will take on some interesting forms as we look to 2014 and beyond. It will no longer be relegated to the traditional factor of race/ethnicity. With the passage of the Americans with Disabilities Act (ADA) of 1990 and the ADA Amendments Act of 2008, the concept of disability should be on the radar screen for most, if not all, Americans. It is a form of disadvantaged status that arguably comes with its own subjective reality or worldview (i.e., cultural bias) that can be a generic viewpoint synonymous to disability status in general or specific to particular types of disability. We also know that persons without a disability may possess a bias toward those who have disabilities. For example, the phenomenon of stigma is well-documented in the disability world.

Beyond disability status, we are seeing more mainstreaming of the gay and lesbian communities, including bisexual and transgendered individuals. With this comes a greater acceptance of people expressing who they truly are and their lifestyle preferences. Same-sex marriages are becoming more widely acceptable in the American landscape. With greater acceptance on the one hand, there will always be some stigmatization or cultural bias on the other hand from certain factions of the American populace.

We will begin to see more cultural bias targeted to individuals who have multiple different or disadvantaged statuses. For example, I have a colleague at the California State University in Fresno, Dr. Jenelle Pitt, who has written about the Triple Threat phenomenon of disability, racial or ethnic minority status, and poverty. Persons who have these three statuses concurrently comprise a group of disadvantaged individuals in which the cultural bias might be multidimensional.

It is clear to me that we face some uncharted waters ahead and that these new developments will afford ample opportunity for us to see that we are all still racists because I predict that cultural bias will be as pervasive as ever. Each new spin on how one's individuality can manifest has the likelihood to threaten or challenge each of our subjective realities, cultural sensibilities, and sense of what seems normal. These responses will all be natural since nothing has occurred that changes our humanness.

One thing is for sure. The pluralistic attribute of American society along with the individual freedoms that our constitution guarantees ensure that the four processes of *enculturation* (learning own culture from significant others), *acculturation* (taking on some cultural characteristics of mainstream America while maintaining strong ties to own indigenous culture), *assimilation* (assuming the cultural traits of a new, more dominant culture and giving up own indigenous culture), and *amalgamation* (a blending of own and a new cultural orientation to constitute an entirely different cultural perspective) will be alive and well as we go forward.

Speaking of going forward, the jury is still out on a few key topics that might shed some light on how cultural bias continues to shape our American realities. It will be interesting to see how the legacy of the Obama presidency is characterized in both the minds of United States citizens and in history books. Of additional interest will be learning how the narrative on immigration reform takes shape as this issue is one that has a direct interface with cultural orientation and continues to be a challenge with which our nation grapples.

## STILL NOT CONVINCED THAT WE ARE ALL RACISTS (I.E., CULTURAL BIAS AFFECTS EACH OF US)?

If you are still not convinced of the power and pervasiveness of cultural bias in our current society, I want you to consider two examples not focused on the dimension of race. First, let's look at the dimension of religion. Why is it so difficult for two black men of the same socioeconomic and educational status to see eye to eye on the existential meaning of life and man's role when one is a Black Muslim and the other is a Southern Baptist? Their experiences in America and worldviews are very comparable on almost all dimensions except the religious one. This difference in spiritual worldview can render these two men light-years apart in how they view the world. This is an example of cultural bias as seen through the prism of the dimension of religious difference.

In the second example, think about two affluent white men. Both are well educated formally as attorneys and are members of our United States Congress. They occupy the same socioeconomic strata. The difference is that one is a conservative Republican who believes in states' rights, a small federal government, and that because America is the land of opportunity, all citizens can pull themselves up by their proverbial bootstraps. The other is a liberal Democrat and believes that though America is the land of opportunity, those opportunities are not evenly distributed for all people based on birth rights. This individual believes in the crippling effect of poverty and past societal discrimination and knows that the United States playing field is never truly level for all people. Consequently, this individual is not opposed to government intervention and having government programs and safeguards in place to ensure equitable access and equality of opportunity for those who are disadvantaged.

Both of these men, though so much alike on many dimensions, are so different on political party affiliation and worldview that they can hardly stand to be in each others' company. This is the power of cultural bias, and in this case, that bias is rooted in political party affiliation. The differences ideologically along their respective party lines are so stark, they believe they have virtually nothing in common beyond the fact that both are United States citizens and congressmen.

These two brief examples, hopefully, shed some light on the power of cultural bias, albeit not bias based on race or ethnicity, but rather the dimensions of religion and political affiliation. Okay, if you are still not convinced that we/you are racist and that cultural bias affects you personally, let's do a short exercise. The exercise is called "How Diverse Is Your World?"

## HOW DIVERSE IS YOUR WORLD?[6]

For each question below, please answer honestly by indicating a primary diversity description for each response (i.e., indicate the predominant or numerical majority of the race or ethnicity that fits your answer). No one will see your results so be as candid with yourself as possible.

1. Who are you married to or who do you date mostly?
2. Who are your best friends?
3. Who are you likely to invite to your home for dinner or on a holiday?
4. Who do you socialize with on a regular basis?
5. Who do you worship with?
6. Who are you likely to eat lunch with on a regular basis at work or school?

7.  If your family took a vacation with another family, how would you describe the other family?
8.  Who is the ideal person for your son or daughter to marry? (If you don't have children, answer as if you did.)
9.  Describe who you are least likely to fear in a dark alley.
10. If you had to sit with a group of complete strangers while dining in a new restaurant, describe the group with whom you would be most comfortable sitting?

Notice the diversity themes related to race or ethnicity that are pervasive in your responses to the ten questions above. If your descriptions in a majority of questions (at least six questions) match who you are in terms of race or ethnicity, then your world is not very diverse, even though we live in a pluralistic society. If your descriptions in a majority of questions do not match who you are in terms of race or ethnicity, then your world is pretty diverse. For those of you with a pretty diverse world, you probably have less cultural bias in terms of race or ethnicity, though you are not entirely devoid of it.

As you may have surmised, the point of the above exercise is to see the extent to which an individual chooses to be in diverse company in those life contexts where we have control over whom with which we interface. My thought is that because we live in the United States, a very diverse nation, most people live under the illusion that they lead a lifestyle that is characterized by cultural diversity. That is, we may have interactions with individuals of other cultures, but I submit this is mostly a function of being in situations where we have not selected the persons with whom we interact, e.g., job or school settings. In situations where we do control who we interface with, I propose that most of us choose those with whom we are most comfortable, and as humans, that tends to be people of same race/ethnicity. This brief exercise is designed to see where one falls in such situations.

## GOOD NEWS

So should we be surprised that by and large, whites and blacks view the George Zimmerman verdict, the Michael Dunn verdict, or even the O. J. Simpson case outcome differently? I think not. It is, after all, another expression of cultural bias, which is a human trait. We are all, to the extent that we are influenced by cultural bias (and we all are), racists. And though this aforementioned statement sounds like a heavy indictment of us, I hope it is clear now from this discussion that it really is not. We are all racists, especially at the level of being animals in that we tend to prefer our own. However, the good news is that as human beings, we have the ability to be volitional. It is this uniquely human quality that allows us to rise above the "animalistic" function and make choices that render us non-racists.

There are no indictments and there is considerable good news. First, America was conceived and built on the premise of facing challenges and the unknown with courage and tenacity. Secondly, Americans have almost always feared change on the surface while embracing it all the while. As noted futurist, Joel Barker, stated in his 1993 book, *Paradigms: the Business of Discovering the Future*, though Americans have not often outwardly embraced change, our behavior has demonstrated that we are accustomed to it. He notes the dramatic change in America between 1890 and 1910 with such advancements as the invention of the radio, the first car was built, air travel began, the cause of malaria was discovered, Einstein proved the theory of relativity, and x-rays as well as electric lights and electrons were discovered. Those were profound discoveries. Think about how different life would be today if any one of them had not been made?

Thomas Kuhn in his 1970 book, *The Structure of Scientific Revolution,* speaks about the fact that humans are always resistant initially to new things because our current mind-set (i.e., the status quo) blocks us from being open to new ideas. We will all continue to be human, but know that as a society, America has always exhibited resilience in adjusting to change. Furthermore, America has always depended on having a cadre of people who were trailblazers, noble and bold enough to rise about their cultural biases and the pervasive attitudes of the day to "do the right thing." I am talking about people like President Abraham Lincoln, the 1954 United States Supreme Court justices, President Lyndon B. Johnson, and the citizenry that elected Barack Obama in 2008 and again in 2012. We shall overcome…everything, but our humanness.

## CULMINATING COMMENT

I have attempted to do several things in this discussion. First, I provided a bit of my own personal history in the interest of being transparent about what got me to this point of making the assertion that this book makes: that we are all racists. My point in telling the story of those personal experiences was to demonstrate that my life experiences were typical and that they have shaped me into the person that I am today. As one could see from my early experiences, I grew up in a wholesome, healthy, loving, value-anchored household, yet there was some bias in my life. I submit that most Americans are the same in this regard. Beyond this personal account, I attempted to provide a somewhat formal discussion about the nature of cultural bias, ultimately making the point, hopefully, that as human beings we cannot help but be biased due to the natural human processes of cognitive schemas and subjective reality.

Next, I talked about what the past tells us. In introducing this topic, my hope was to move the discussion of cultural bias to a larger, more macro-societal level within the United States landscape. I focused primarily on the black versus white dynamic that has and continues to plague America. Hopefully, my discussion of the periods of black advancement followed by periods of white backlash conveyed the cyclical, long-term, and sustainable nature of the cultural bias between these two groups over time. I, then, briefly addressed the cultural bias that has occurred in this nation against some other traditional racial and ethnic minority groups.

Subsequently, I focused on community healing and offered the black community as an example of the type of healing that is needed in order for blacks to be able to mitigate to some extent their cultural bias. As an exemplar, the discussion about the black community was intended to both be an illustration of the complexity of challenges involved as well as provide an up-close and personal perspective on the black condition, which has been the subject of discussion in this country for many decades. My treatment of the black condition addressed: a data perspective on the current status of blacks in America, the black community psyche and its current trauma-induced state along with some reasons, the presidency of Barack Obama as a potential illustration of the current white backlash phenomenon, and two illustrations from my own life experience that demonstrate the magnitude of the challenge of refocusing our youth. I then offered a remedy for the psychological trauma experienced by the black community in the form of ten self-help strategies for community enhancement in the Black Triangle.

Finally, I ended the discussion on a positive note by looking forward to the future. In doing so, I spent a little time talking about the black community health imperative, which arguably could have been part of the previous chapter on the black community. I decided to isolate it as a stand-alone challenge to give it adequate attention. In addition to this, I presented some interesting developments that are currently occurring that relate to cultural bias and really point to new manifestations of bias. For those who are still not convinced about the power and pervasiveness of cultural bias, I provided two brief illustrations that relate to religious and political bias and then introduced a short self-evaluation exercise. The discussion concluded addressing several points that constitute good news going forward, namely that America was built on addressing challenges and exhibiting resilience and that we have a history that provides a legacy of the country's success in this regard. I hope that you have gained something positive from this discussion. I certainly gained from having written it.

# REFERENCES

Addison, K. N. (2009). *"We hold these truths to be self-evident..."*: *An interdisciplinary analysis of the roots of racism and slavery in America.* Lanham, MD: University Press of America, Inc.

Adorno, T. W., Frenkel-Brunswik, E., Levinson, D. J., & Sanford, R. N. (1950). *The authoritarian personality.* New York, NY: Harper Brothers.

Atkinson, D. R., Morten, G., & Sue, D. W. (1998). *Counseling American minorities.* Boston, MA: McGraw-Hill.

Bandura, A. (1971). *Social learning theory.* New York, NY: General Learning Press.

Brown, R. (1965). *Social psychology.* New York, NY: Free Press.

Chapman, R. J. (1988). Cultural Bias in Alcoholism Counseling. Retrieved on February 9, 2011. http://www. robertchapman.net/essays/bias.htm.

Cherry, K. (2011). Background and key concepts of Piaget's theory: Stages of cognitive development. Retrieved February 10, 2011. http://psychology.about.com/od/piagetstheory/a/keyconcepts.htm.

Fujiura, G. T., & Drazen, C. (2009). "Ways of seeing" in race and disability research. In *Race, culture, and disability: Rehabilitation science and practice* (Eds.) Balcazar, F. E., Suarez- Balcazar, Y., Taylor-Ritzler, T., & Keys, C.B. Boston, MA: Jones and Bartlett Publishers, 15-32.

Gardenswartz, L., & Rowe, A., (1998). *Managing diversity in health care.* San Francisco, CA: Jossey-Bass.

Hahn, H. (1988). Can disability be beautiful? *Social Policy,* 18(3), 26–32.

Heilbronner, R.L. (2011). Bias. In *Encyclopedia of Clinical Neuropsychology,* (Eds.) Kreutzer, J. S., Deluca, J., & Caplan, B. New York, NY: Springer Science and Business Media, LLC, 2, 400-401.

Huntington, L. (1999 spring semester). How do humans make sense of diversity? Disability, Development and Diversity, RHAB 654. Class Lecture. Virginia Commonwealth University.

Laudan, L. (2006). *Truth, error, and criminal law: An essay in legal epistemology.* New York, NY: Cambridge University Press.

Lefley, H.P. (2002). Ethical issues in mental health services for culturally diverse populations. In *Ethics in Community Mental Health Care* (Eds.) Backlar P., Cutler D. L. New York, NY: Kluwer Academic/Plenum, 3-22.

Lewis, A.N. (2006). The Three-factor model of multicultural counseling for consumers with disabilities. *Journal of Vocational Rehabilitation,* 24(3), 151-159.

Lewis, A.N., & Shamburger, A. (2009). A Three-dimensional model for multicultural rehabilitation counseling. In *Race, culture and disability: Rehabilitation science and practice* (Eds.) Balcazar, F., Suarez-Balcazar, Y., Taylor-

Ritzler, T., & Keys, C. Boston, MA: Jones and Bartlett, 229-253.

Maynard, M. & Purvis, J. (2002). *Researching women's lives from a Feminist perspective*. New York, NY: Taylor & Francis.

Nichols, E. J. (1989). *The philosophical aspects of cultural difference.* Unpublished paper delivered at The Evergreen State College, Tacoma, Washington.

Pedersen, P. B. (2008). Ethics, competence, and professional issues in cross-cultural counseling. In *Counseling across Cultures* (Eds.) Pendersen, P. B., Draguns, J. G., Lonner, W. J., & Trimble, J. E.). Thousand Oaks, CA: Sage Publications, Inc., 5-20.

Pedersen, P. B. (1987). Ten frequent assumptions of cultural bias in counseling. *Journal of Multicultural Counseling and Development*, 15, 16-22.

Piaget, J. (1972). *The psychology of the child.* New York, NY: Basic Books.

Schaffer, R. T. (1988). *Racial and ethnic groups* (3rd Ed.). Glenview, IL: Scott, Foresman and Company.

Sherif, M. (1964). *Reference groups: Exploration into conformity and deviation of adolescents.* Scranton, PA: HarperCollins College Division.

Sumner, W. G. (1960). *Folkways.* New York, NY: Mentor Books.

Trochim, W. M. The Research Methods Knowledge Base (2nd Ed.). Retrieved on February 5, 2011 from http://www. socialresearchmethods.net/kb/ (version current as of October 20, 2006).

Turner, J. C., Brown, R. J., & Tajfel, H. (1979). Social comparison and group interest in in-group favoritism. *European Journal of Social Psychology*, 9, 187–204.

Usher, C.H. (1989). Recognizing cultural bias in counseling theory and practice: The case of Rogers. *Journal of Multicultural Counseling and Development*, 17(2), 62-71.

Van Dijk, T. A. (1993). *Elite discourse and racism.* Newbury Park, CA: Sage.

Walker, I., & Smith, H. J. (2002). *Relative deprivation: Specification, development and integration.* Cambridge, UK: Cambridge University Press.

Yuker, H. (1965). Attitudes as determinants of behavior. *Journal of Rehabilitation, 31,* 5–16.

# NOTES

1. This number is based on an approximate US population of 300 million and an estimated 13 percent black population.
2. This number is based on the 2007 Federal Reserve's Survey of Consumer Finances that indicates the top 1 percent of black families in the United States earn on average at least $800K/year. This number makes it seem like the top 1 percent of blacks are pretty affluent, and they are. However, keep in mind that the mean income of black families in the top 1 percent is 22 percent less than white families in the top 1 percent, and blacks make up 1.4 percent of the nation's top 1 percent; whites comprise 96.2 percent.
3. This is according to a 2012 ranking of US cities based on actual 2010 population data from the US Census Bureau and estimated 2012 population data. There are actually 289 incorporated US cities with populations of at least 100,000 people, but I used the number 300 for convenience and simplicity.
4. Keep in mind that this number might be a little bit conservative because it is based on 2007 data and it is

the lower bound of the average income of blacks in the top 1 percent.

5. Using disability as a sub-domain within general health, my model offers a beginning framework for understanding the concept of disability disparities. It is designed to convey the continuum along which the experience of having a disability, which is much like having a chronic health condition, can be different for culturally diverse populations from the point of occurrence of disability (i.e., incidence) to outcomes of services. This continuum represents a five-domain progression that is indicative of a natural flow from a racial or ethnic minority individual's initial engagement with the formal disability system if that individual's cultural group desires to receive services in the system to the point of having realized some outcomes. The progression includes: Domain 1: incidence of disability, Domain 2: contemplation about participation in the formal system, Domain 3: accessing the formal system once a decision is made to do so, Domain 4: level of participation once in the formal system, and Domain 5: the individual level outcomes achieved as facilitated by the formal system of services.

Depicted at the top of the model is a set of five factors that constitute a hypothesized view of what accounts for the differential experiences of culturally diverse populations along the five-domain progression that ranges from beginning interaction with the formal rehabilitation and disability system to the point of impact. These five factors are logical explanations that attempt to provide a rationale for and begin to explain why disability disparities exist. The model is also comprised of macro- and micro-level components that address the same aforementioned five-domain continuum.

On the macro-level, the five domains on the continuum specify that the concept of disability disparity can take on five distinct forms. While the macro-aspect of the model attempts to offer conceptual clarity on the phenomenon of disability disparities, as in promoting the precise understanding and discernment required for individuals conducting disability disparities research, the micro-aspect of the model provides hints to practitioners regarding specific considerations to explore when working with actual individuals with disabilities who are members of racial and ethnic minority groups. On the micro-level, the options for exploration correspond to the same five domains on the continuum as the macro-level.

The general health disparity literature indicates that culture influences service outcomes. According to the Institute of Medicine (Smedley, Stith, and Nelson, 2003), health disparities are disproportionately negative outcomes seen in racial and ethnic minority groups even when factors such as access and socioeconomic status are controlled. The Institute of Medicine reports several hundred studies published between the years of 1992 and 2002 that document the existence of racial and ethnic health disparities (Smedley, Stith, and Nelson, 2003).

An assumption inherent in this model is that a different pattern of experiences endemic to groups that are culturally different from the majority population (i.e., whites) in each of the five domains on the continuum is undesirable. For example, with Domain 1, the model assumes that a higher incidence of disability among racial and ethnic minority groups compared to non-minority groups is something that ethnic minority groups want to remedy. However, it may be somewhat presumptuous to assume that a group with higher incidence of a particular disability wants to lower that rate of morbidity to something that is more in line with the occurrence of disability in other groups (i.e., majority group populations). This simply may not be the case, and therefore, it could be a faulty assumption that anchors this model. If so, this assumption may need to be explored with each cultural group to which this model is applied.

6.  These questions were modified from an earlier iteration of a set of questions originally developed by Marian Martin at the University of Virginia in 2002.

7.  Portions of the chapter titled "Cultural Bias is Real" have been reproduced from previous publications written by this author with permission from those publishers:

a.  Journal of Minority Disability Research and Practice at Texas Southern University, article titled: *Anatomy of Cultural Bias and Strategies to Overcome It* (2011)

b.  Aspen Professional Services, chapter titled: *The Multicultural Rehabilitation Counseling Imperative in the 21st Century* (2012) in the book New Directions in Rehabilitation Counseling: Creative Responses to Professional, Clinical, and Educational Challenges

8.  The Lewis Disability Disparities Model (2009) that appears near the beginning of the chapter titled "Looking Forward" has been reproduced with permission from the 2009 journal article titled "Disability Disparities: A Beginning Model" written by this author and that appeared in the journal Disability and Rehabilitation that is published by Informal Healthcare. The content that comprises discussion of attributes of the model in note 5 above is also taken from the journal article published by this author.